'the eighth wonder of the world'

EXBURY GARDENS AND THE ROTHSCHILDS

'the eighth wonder of the world'

EXBURY GARDENS AND THE ROTHSCHILDS

Lionel de Rothschild and Francesca Murray Rowlins

many I have never received at all. I should be very grateful for any of these, but especially for the Rhodo. and Primula series.

I see no chance of getting up to Scotland till the autumn now. I have just spent a very delightful week end at Mr. Lionel Rothschild's place – he has a marvellous display of Rhodos. Within 5 years it will be the eighth wonder of the world.

I have to go down to Torquay in June, and over to Ireland in May. All the same I am very much looking forward to a visit to Scotland, and would have been delighted to come next month if irresistible pressure had not been brought to bear.

There are simply dozens of things I want to ask you, but I forebear – it really isn't fair, so I will wait till I can ask

The title of this book is taken from a letter written by plant hunter Frank Kingdon-Ward (1885–1958) addressed to the Keeper of the Royal Botanic Garden Edinburgh on 24 April 1923. Exbury, he says, will be 'the eighth wonder of the world'.

opposite title page · R. 'Fortune'

left · R. magnificum (KW 9200), a Kingdon-Ward introduction at Exbury

Text by Lionel de Rothschild and Francesca Murray Rowlins

CONTENTS

Magnolias, *see page 196*

The interwar years in the first half of the last century were an exceptional period of plant discovery and garden creation led, in this country, by a dedicated cadre of wealthy enthusiasts, foremost of whom was Lionel de Rothschild. His tastes were eclectic, but his first love was for rhododendrons – a passion which he pursued with uncommon energy. His ambition was to create a horticultural paradise in which to showcase the newly discovered species being brought back from the Sino-Himalayas and other far-flung regions (together with the many hybrids he made from them) in the company of an extraordinary range of other rare trees and shrubs.

Lionel's vision was realised in the remarkably short period of twenty years, but he will only have seen the Gardens in their infancy. Now they are in their full maturity, having been augmented over the years by his sons and further generations of his family, and have proved a source of great joy to many thousands of visitors ever since they were opened to the public over sixty years ago. It is, I think, important to recall the enormous contribution made by Edmund de Rothschild in securing Exbury Gardens' future after his father, Lionel, died in 1942. Edmund was a great pillar of the horticultural world and, like his father, he was a recipient of the prestigious Royal Horticultural Society's Victoria Medal of Honour.

Now, more than ever, people are realising the benefits, both mental as well as physical, of being surrounded by beauty in the open air. I know how much peace and pleasure I, like countless others, find in my own garden. I also know, together with other members of my family who have had the good fortune to visit Exbury on various occasions, what a joy it is to wander through that 'horticultural paradise', overcome with admiration for its founder's exquisite legacy to us all.

We should be grateful that Lionel's grandson, and namesake, has now written this history of Exbury Gardens – 'the eighth wonder of the world'. It is a story which richly deserves to be told.

INTRODUCTION

Every year Exbury Gardens welcomes tens of thousands of visitors. Most come to enjoy their beauty and the enormous collection of rare plants, trees and shrubs that are set in a spacious landscape; few, however, will be aware of the extraordinary story of their creation at the hands of Lionel de Rothschild in the first half of the last century. It is a romantic story of a man who had the energy and single-minded determination to push the boundaries of horticulture by financing the discovery of new species and by breeding new hybrids from their seeds.

It was a happy coincidence that Lionel's interest developed at a time when new areas of the world were being explored by intrepid plant hunters, and when competition was provided by a number of other ambitious men eager to enjoy the treasures these plant hunters sent back. It was also fortunate that Lionel had the means to pursue his passion with such vigour. Readers of this book will marvel at the fact that he achieved so much in just the 20 years between his purchase of the Exbury Estate in 1919 and the outbreak of the Second World War in 1939.

Crucially, Lionel was interested not just in his plants but also in where and how they were planted. His genius lies in the way he incorporated them into the natural landscape he found at Exbury so as to create a setting and an ambience which delights even those who know little about horticulture. He had an artist's eye and a scientist's brain and it shows.

This book is principally about Exbury Gardens – 'the eighth wonder of the world' – but it is also about the members of the Rothschild family who created it and who continue to direct and support it into its second century. After Lionel's early death, the baton was taken up first by his widow, Marie-Louise, and then successively by his sons Edmund and Leopold. The family interest now extends to members of the third and fourth generations, all of whom – together with a dedicated team of employees and volunteers – are committed to the conservation and development of these remarkable gardens and to sharing their treasures.

Marcus Agius, Chairman, Exbury Gardens Limited

Frost on *R. glischroides* · *previous page*, R. 'Mrs Lionel de Rothschild'

left
The five Rothschild brothers. Lithograph by Hermann Raunheim after portraits by Moritz Daniel Oppenheim, Paris 1852. Clockwise from the top: Amschel, Salomon, Carl, James and Nathan.

opposite, above
Lionel de Rothschild (1808–1879) was the eldest of Nathan's sons. After his father's death he ran the London bank in partnership with his brothers and is remembered for advancing the funds required by the British Government to acquire shares in the Suez Canal in 1875 as well as his successful campaign to become the first Jewish MP.

below
Lionel de Rothschild (1882–1942)

The Rothschild family at Exbury

Lionel de Rothschild (1882–1942) bought the Exbury estate in 1919. He was the great-grandson of Nathan Mayer Rothschild who had arrived in Britain from Frankfurt in 1798, working firstly in Manchester as a textile merchant before moving to London around 1808. Nathan was the third of five Rothschild brothers who established banking houses in Frankfurt, London, Paris, Vienna and Naples during the late eighteenth and early nineteenth centuries.

Mayer Amschel Rothschild 1744–1812 = (1770) Gutle Schnapper 1753–1849

Nathan Mayer
1777–1836
= 1806
Hannah Barent Cohen
1783–1850

Isabella
1781–1861

Babette
1784–1869

Carl Mayer
1788–1855

Julie
1790–1815

Henriette
1791–1866

James Mayer
1792–1868

Lionel
1808–1879
= 1836
Charlotte von
Rothschild
1819–1884

below
Leopold de Rothschild and his wife, Marie.
The youngest of Lionel's five children, he
developed the family's gardens at Gunnersbury
and at Ascott, Buckinghamshire.

Leopold (*far right*)
1845–1917
= 1881
Marie Perugia
1862–1937

13

Lionel
1882–1942
= 1912
Marie-Louise Beer
(Mariloo)
1892–1975

Evelyn Achille
1886–1917

Anthony Gustav
1887–1961
= 1926
Yvonne Cahen d'Anvers
1899–1977
issue

Rosemary
1913–2013
= [1] 1934
Denis Berry
1911–1983
= [2] 1942
Antony Seys
1914–1989
issue

Edmund (Eddy)
(*right*)
1916–2009
= [1] 1948
Elizabeth Lentner
1923–1980
= [2] 1982
Anne Harrison
1921–2012

Naomi
1920–2007
= [1] 1941
Jean-Pierre Reinach
1915–1942
= [2] 1947
Bertrand Goldschmidt
1912–2002
issue

Leopold (Leo)
(*far right*)
1927–2012

Katherine (Kate)
b.1949
= 1971
Marcus Agius
b.1946

Nicholas (Nick)
b.1951
= 1985
Caroline Darvall
b.1955

Charlotte
b.1955
= 1990
Nigel Brown
1936–2021

Lionel
b.1955
= 1991
Louise Williams
b.1955

Marie-Louise
b.1977

Lara
b.1980
= 2010
Samuel
Smith-Bosanquet
b.1980
issue

Chloë
b.1990

Elizabeth
b.1992

Leopold
b.1994

Amschel
b.1995

Before Exbury

THE ROTHSCHILD GARDENERS

CHAPTER 1

This is a book about one of England's best-known and best-loved gardens. But the story begins more than 150 years before the gardens at Exbury were created in a rather different – and much more limited – environment.

Many books and articles have been written about the Rothschild family, the descendants of Mayer Amschel Rothschild, a merchant in Frankfurt in the late eighteenth century. He was initially forced to operate within the confines of the city's Jewish ghetto. Despite this, Mayer Amschel became a trusted agent of William I, Elector of Hesse (1743–1821) and his reputation spread throughout Europe.

After his death his five sons, partners with him from 1810, began to establish business houses across the continent. By 1820 there were Rothschild businesses in London, Paris, Vienna and Naples, as well as Frankfurt. The Rothschild family of Exbury are descended from the third of Mayer Amschel's sons, Nathan Mayer Rothschild, who was the first to leave Frankfurt. He arrived in England in 1798 aged 21, first operating as a merchant in Manchester. Just over a decade later he became a London banker, settling into premises in New Court, St Swithin's Lane, in 1809. He developed the business further by arranging bills of exchange and foreign loans and, significantly, in 1814 he was commissioned by the British government to help fund the campaign of the allies against Napoleon. A year later this culminated in the Battle of Waterloo. The firm that his descendants inherited is still based in New Court and is still led by members of the Rothschild family.

Much of this is well known. Less well known is the Rothschilds' role in the development and evolution of gardening. Their first foray came about in a rather unusual way. Their prominence in European society as a result of their business success enabled the family to take an active role in campaigning for the rights of Jewish minorities. The Jewish community in Frankfurt had been granted the right to acquire land outside the ghetto – a privilege extended by Napoleon Bonaparte; however, it was in danger of being rescinded by the Frankfurt city fathers in the wake of Napoleon's defeat. Previously this right had been denied; indeed Jews were barred from walking in public parks. The Rothschilds helped to secure the right to acquire land and decided to make a purchase: a house was deemed too showy, so the brothers agreed that Amschel, the oldest, should buy a garden.

In May 1816 Amschel reported with delight: 'I bought the garden this morning, with God's help, since you have all written several times to do so. From today the garden belongs to me and my dear brothers ... this garden is a family inheritance.' It was something to which they all contributed and which Nathan regarded as a 'necessity as much as bread', an indication perhaps of how important gardens were to him and his brothers – and would be to their descendants.

Amschel hoped his brother Salomon would 'provide some nice seeds or plants at the earliest opportunity', as he believed the garden was a direct contributor to his good health and would sleep in it at night to alleviate the headaches that plagued him. 'I slept at the garden for the first time today. It was halfway to being the Garden of Eden'.

Buying a garden was not the only first for Amschel; he was also the first member of the family to invest in a glasshouse. Despite the limitations faced by gardening enthusiasts of the time, the brothers kept up a regular exchange of the latest exotic plants and seeds using their international network of business agents, many of whom were encouraged to act as informal plant hunters.

In the generations that followed, the family's increased wealth and influence ensured that they could acquire and build houses that would become showcases for their collections of pictures, porcelain and furniture. The English Rothschild houses such as Mentmore Towers, Tring Park, Halton House, Ascott and Waddesdon Manor, all clustered round the Vale of Aylesbury, became well known for their stylish entertaining. The family's hospitality and their keenness to embrace English culture went some way towards breaking down social and political barriers.

Along with their houses they also acquired, restored and designed gardens; in fact, by now gardening was in their blood.

Mentmore from S.W.

opposite
Ascott House, showing the lawns
and topiary peacock

clockwise from top left
Mentmore Towers; the Winter
Garden at Halton House; Halton
House; Waddesdon Manor;
bedding schemes at Ascott House

previous pages · see page 197

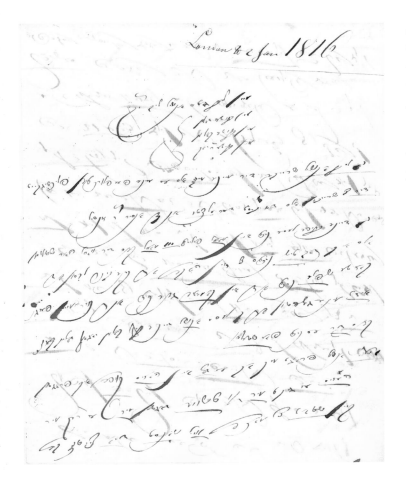

grown by their expert head gardeners. They also embraced the opportunity to support scientific experimentation and invest in the latest advances in gardening. They clearly took it all very seriously but at the same time, the gardens, glasshouses, and plants were a pleasurable distraction from the demands of business.

In 1835 Nathan Rothschild acquired an estate in Gunnersbury, west of London, with substantial gardens, although his death just a year later meant that it was his widow, Hannah and their children who benefited most from its pleasures. Their son Lionel inherited Gunnersbury and a share of his father's personal fortune. In all, four generations of English Rothschilds lived at Gunnersbury Park, which became the heart of family life and saw the continuation of the dynastic devotion to horticulture.

The attraction of Gunnersbury Park was that it was close enough to London and already an established estate. Of course, the Rothschilds were not the first owners to make their mark on it. It appeared on the Rocque map of 1746, one of the earliest detailed maps of London. That illustration shows a formal garden, two narrow ponds and an *allée* of trees but between 1740 and 1785 this was extended using the natural landscaping style of the time. The eminent architects William Kent (1685–1748) and William Chambers (1723–1796) are known to have worked at Gunnersbury and may have designed the Round Pond, Temple and surrounding plantings of 'fine cedars', which were noted by visitors throughout the ensuing centuries. The Horseshoe Pond was formed soon after this and further buildings added in the park.

Previously, in 1760, Gunnersbury had become the country estate of Princess Amelia (1711–1786) a favourite daughter of George II, and she would live there for the rest of her life. The Royal Family was known to love gardens, owning many of England's finest, and the Gunnersbury grounds were said to have been 'greatly improved by her Royal Highness, to which many Additions were made by Plantations, additional ground and elegant erections', including a rustic grotto and pool adorned with seashells. In 1801 the land had been split into two, thus creating two separate estates, each with a new house, the so-called 'Large Mansion' as Gunnersbury Park and the 'Small Mansion' as Gunnersbury House. Each was built in close proximity to the other, though separated by a wall, on the elevated position of a terrace overlooking the Horseshoe Pond. They were not to be formally reunited for nearly a century.

That said, an interest in the latest horticultural trends was an inevitable pastime of a rich and influential family who shared their style outside as much as inside their country houses.

By landscaping their gardens with fashionable features and planting them with the latest exotic plants arriving from distant shores, the Rothschilds now joined the company of other enthusiastic gardeners who owned country estates of a similar size and stature. They enjoyed competing with their peers to win prizes for their horticultural produce and hothouse plants

above
Letter from Nathan Rothschild advising Amschel to buy a garden rather than a house

opposite
Autochrome picture by Lionel of his father, Leo, by the lily pond at Gunnersbury

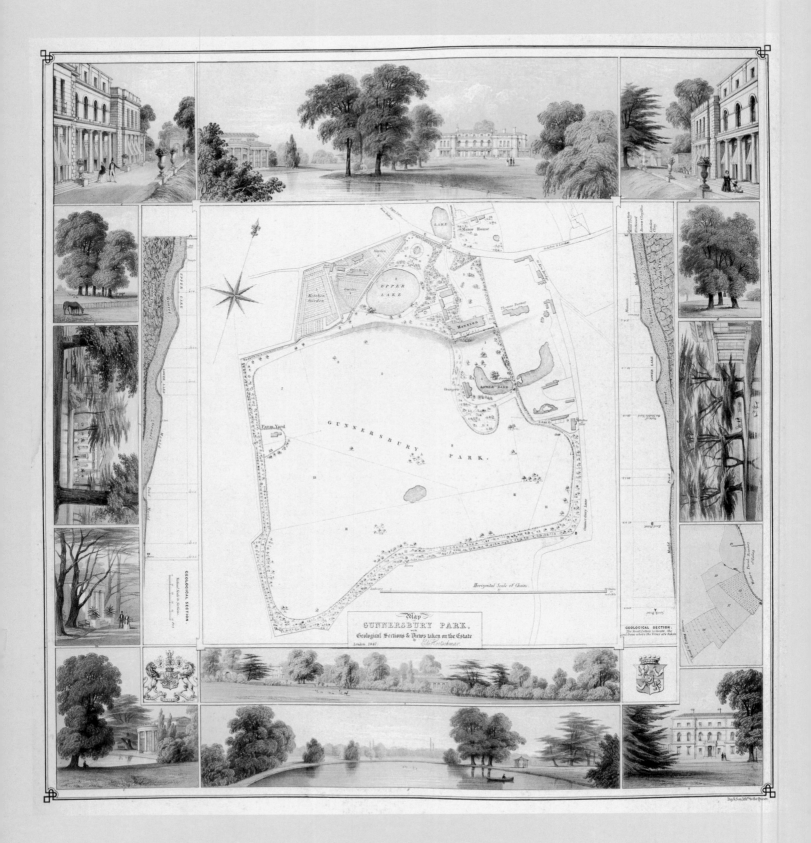

Map
GUNNERSBURY PARK,
with
Geological Sections & Views taken on the Estate

London 1847.

At Gunnersbury Park, Lionel and his wife Charlotte derived much pleasure from the gardens: Charlotte's invitations were much sought after and the garden tour was a special feature of the guests' entertainment. Strawberries and exotic fruit – particularly pineapples ('pines') and melons – grown by their talented head gardener, William Forsyth, were given as gifts. In 1874, *The Gardeners' Chronicle* reported that while Gunnersbury Park should be famous for its pines 'of superior excellence', it should also be as famous for its cool-loving orchids, grown with such 'skilful and enthusiastic management' by John Richards, the orchid grower and Forsyth's eventual successor.

Charlotte had a keen interest in gardening and published a catalogue of the Gunnersbury orchids in a small pamphlet, listing 237 orchids and in each case giving the name, meaning of the name and country of origin. She frequently presented prizes – and planted a few commemorative trees – at the local Ealing, Acton and Hanwell Horticultural Society and the Jews' Free School, then in Spitalfields in the east end of London. New trees, often sizeably mature, were introduced by the Rothschilds and arranged in the parkland where the family rode their horses. Charlotte and her eldest son Nathaniel, known as 'Natty', regularly visited the trade nurseries to view the latest imports from all parts of the world. In 1865 she wrote to her son Leo of one such visit, 'The perfume of the orchids was quite heavenly – and several novelties from distant lands arrested our attention.' The plants they saw arrived in Wardian cases – sealed protective containers for plants, invented by Dr Nathaniel Bagshaw Ward (1791–1868) – to protect them during the long sea voyage.

The Rothschilds even had an influence on the garden supply industry: they became early patrons of the plant nursery James Veitch & Sons, which had opened in Chelsea in 1853; Veitch went on to become a preferred supplier to many of the richest houses of England.

A hand-coloured lithograph of 1847 shows twelve views of the mansion and park and reveals what it would have looked like as the family settled in. In a vignette near the top right a bell can be seen hanging from the trees: Lionel must have been fond of this, as he brought it with him from Gunnersbury and it now hangs at Exbury. The Orangery, Temple, ponds, imposing cedars and mature plantings show an impressive garden and grounds. Among the changes they instigated, the Rothschilds set about transforming an old tile kiln and a pit into a Gothic folly and the Potomac Lake, respectively, at the south side; they also installed

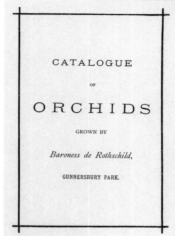

CATALOGUE

OF

ORCHIDS

GROWN BY

Baroness de Rothschild,

GUNNERSBURY PARK.

opposite
Map of Gunnersbury Park, showing a range of views, by E. Kretschmar, 1847

left and above
Charlotte's catalogue of orchids; Veitch were one of their favoured suppliers

new vineries and glasshouses. The family addressed their improvements with great energy and attention to detail.

On Lionel's death in 1879 his three sons inherited the estate. However it was his youngest son Leopold (Leo) who settled there. Much of his time was taken up with his sporting pursuits, hunting at his Ascott estate and horse-racing at Newmarket. Leo was known as 'the most popular owner on the Turf next to His Majesty'.

Like his mother and brother, he was devoted to the interests of horticulture and wanted to make his mark on his gardens. He was also a keen patron of the horticultural community. He was at various times the Vice-President of The Gardeners' Royal Benevolent Institution and The Royal Gardeners' Orphan Fund and he was President of the Jury at the Royal International Horticultural Exhibition held in 1912 on the grounds of the Royal Hospital, Chelsea; this was so successful that it set the seal on using this site for the Chelsea Flower Show thereafter. Leo also maintained the family's close relationship with the Veitch nurseries, commissioning Sir Harry Veitch (1840–1924), to design and plant the gardens at Ascott: the architect, George Devey (1820–1886), remodelled the house in the Tudor style and Veitch was asked to lay out the gardens.

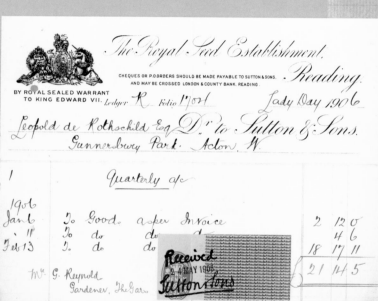

this page
Receipts from The Rothschild Archive show the range of horticultural companies supplying the different Rothschild gardens

opposite · Camellias, see page 196

Knap Hill Nursery, Woking, Surrey.
Near the Woking Station, South Western Railway.

Leopold de Rothschild Esqre.

Bot. of Anthony Waterer

☞ POST OFFICE ORDERS SHOULD BE MADE PAYABLE AT "KNAP HILL"

1906						
Nov 20	500	Begonias pink		3	15	·
1907	500	" white		3	15	·
Mar 5	214	English Yews		26	15	·
	18	Planes		4	10	·
6	106	English Yews		13	5	·
	1	Lime			7	6
	8	Common Hollies		2	·	·
	6	Euonymus radicans variegatus			9	·
	12	Althæa ruby			18	·
	12	" speciosa			18	·
	25	Tamarix Odessana		1	5	·
	2	Solanum Wendlandi			10	·
	6	Cotoneaster Franchetti			9	·
	18	Tritoma erecta			18	·
	30	Roses of sorts		1	2	6
	6	Malus angustifolia fl. pl.			9	·
	2	Euonymus Americana		·	2	·
	2	Prunus Padus Knap Hill variety		·	7	·
		19 July 1907	£	61	15	·

3 S.

The Royal Seed Establishment.
Reading.

BY ROYAL SEALED WARRANT TO KING EDWARD VII.

CHEQUES OR P.O.ORDERS SHOULD BE MADE PAYABLE TO SUTTON & SONS. AND MAY BE CROSSED LONDON & COUNTY BANK. READING.

Ledger K. Folio 1701

Lady Day 1906

Leopold de Rothschild Esq Dr. to Sutton & Sons.
Gunnersbury Park. Acton. W.

Quarterly a/c

1906							
Jan 6	To	Goods	as per Invoice		2	12	0
" 11	To	do	do			4	6
Feb 13	To	do	do		18	17	11
				£	21	14	5

Mr. G. Reynold
Gardener, The Gar...

Received 24 MAY 1906 Sutton & Sons

No. 13051

Telegrams—THOMAS ROCHFORD, WORMLEY, HERTS.

TURNFORD HALL NURSERIES

AND AT 2 & 3, TAVISTOCK STREET, COVENT GARDEN
AND STANDS 258 TO 263, FLOWER MARKET, COVENT GARDEN.
TELEPHONE N° 3577 GERRARD.
PRIVATE TELEPHONE FROM TAVISTOCK ST. TO NURSERIES.

Nr. Broxbourne, Herts,

17th February 1905

Received of Leopold de Rothschild Esq

the Sum of ———— Five ———— Pounds
———— eight ———— Shillings and ———— Pence

Cheque

5 . 8 . 0

For THOMAS ROCHFORD & SONS. LTD

above · View of Gunnersbury House ('the Small Mansion') in Leo's time   *opposite* · Notebook of Thomas Hobbs, giving details of his tasks and planting

Leo was remembered fondly, keen to delegate to his head gardeners and always enormously proud of their gardening efforts, especially when they won prizes at Royal Horticultural Society (RHS) shows. Like his brother Alfred, Leo was especially fond of carnations, orchids and waterlilies. Cut flowers were an essential part of any glasshouse produce and the orchids took centre stage. In 1911, Leo presented orchids from Gunnersbury in a crystal Fabergé vase to King George V on his coronation day.

A notebook surviving from 1893 to 1899 in the hand of one of the gardeners, Thomas Hobbs, listed his various gardening activities in the fig, cherry and orchid houses. A *Vanda teres* (now *Papilionanthe teres*) orchid flowered with over 200 spikes and he cut blooms from it to send to Leo's other houses as well as to family and guests. The south-facing Gunnersbury terrace was the showcase for a very bright – and very fashionable – display of colour with pelargoniums pouring out of evenly placed pots filled with hybrid tea roses and lemon-scented verbenas.

This was the gardening inheritance of Lionel de Rothschild, Leo's eldest son; it was also his inspiration. At the age of five Lionel was given his own little garden at Ascott.

A few years later, in 1889, Leo unified the Gunnersbury estate once more by acquiring the adjoining property of Gunnersbury House; the combined area now ran to some 200 acres. Unusually, he retained the head gardeners of each property and James Hudson (1846–1932), the brilliant head gardener of Gunnersbury House, joined the Rothschild staff. In 1869, while at Deepdene, a woodland garden in Surrey, Hudson had scored top marks in the RHS National Examination in Horticulture, the first ever to do so. In 1897, he was a recipient of the RHS's top honour, the Victoria Medal of Honour (VMH) in the first year of its founding. Overall he was an expert horticulturalist who had perfected the art of propagating and hybridising plants, exhibiting prize-winning fruit and flowers, and mastering hothouse plants.

November 1894

Nov	
1	Group of Plants at the People's Palace
2	Potted Cymbidium eburneum also Callow Little Gem
7	Started potting Carnations cuttings off. New Hot Water pipes in Orange House
9	Azalea got into Vinery
10	Cuttings of Passiflora Kermesina. Coleus. and Asparagus put in. Vanda Kimballiana in flower also Cattleyas Harrisonii Albens. and Bowringeana
13	Bouvardia purity Passiflora Eucharis Sanderiana bought in
Nov 14th	500 Carnations Mrs L de R. potted into rimless 60 old plants from between span

November

Nov	
15	Cleaned & ... House.
16	Passiflora Grevillea ...sima boug...
20	Rose House
23	12 Carnat... Erne bough... Queen Cha...
25	Carnations 100 Mrs L d... Erne + 20 ...
27	Cutbush ... of Carnat... Steamed ...
29	Calla Elli...
30	Begonia G... put in ca... finish t...

Some of the Gunnersbury gardeners

Hudson and Leo had become celebrated hybridisers of water lilies, creating over 50 hybrids, which were displayed in the Horseshoe Pond and in heated tanks beside the glasshouses. The French specialist nursery Latour Marliac supplied waterlilies to Gunnersbury for Hudson, who wanted to use their exceptionally good pollen for hybridising. This surely must have been an inspiration for Lionel.

Over time, Hudson had become an exponent and friend of William Robinson (1838–1935) who famously expressed a loathing for Victorian carpet bedding in his book *The Wild Garden* (1870). Robinson wanted to look with fresh eyes at the old conventions and inspire a new generation with informal planting arrangements, although at a slight distance from the enduring English terrace. He was not alone. A new garden movement, which was endorsed by the renowned horticulturalist and garden designer Gertrude Jekyll (1843–1932), eventually saw the end of the Victorian style of gardening.

Hudson himself wrote extensively: in the *Journal of the Royal Horticultural Society* he talked about the woodland gardens of the Italian lakes around Lake Como, with their rhododendrons and azaleas. Now a young man, Lionel had visited these gardens on his motoring tours of the Continent and Hudson used some of his photographs – Lionel was a keen photographer – to illustrate his articles and lectures.

above
A postcard of the period,
showing the Japanese
Garden at Gunnersbury

previous pages
The Temple at Gunnersbury
with flamingos, another
autochrome by Lionel

During Lionel's youth, Gunnersbury was internationally recognised, with a bamboo garden, heath garden, ivy garden, an Italian garden and the innovative use of new Asiatic woodland plants such as rhododendrons, kalmias and azaleas, which were now arriving in the country. Many people came to see the fashionable new Japanese garden that Hudson created for Leo between 1900 and 1905.

Japanese plants had been quite exclusive but thanks partly to warmer relations between Japan and Britain since the signing, and then the renewal, of the Anglo-Japanese alliance, collectors could send more of them to Europe. Not just Japanese azaleas but water lilies, bamboo and frankly any plant that ended with 'japonica' could be found in an English Japanese garden – even Japanese anemones, which had actually been discovered in China. Sales of replica Japanese garden ornaments – from suppliers such as Gauntletts of Chiddingfold and the Yokohama nursery in St Albans – boomed. At the Japanese gardens in Gatton Park, Surrey, one of the Japanese ornaments was assembled upside down by the head gardener, although no one seemed to notice. With its waterways, small bridges, an elegant tea house, stone lanterns and oriental planting, Gunnersbury's Japanese garden captured the Japanese spirit – or at least was supposed to, though on an official visit the Japanese ambassador remarked, somewhat ambiguously, 'Marvellous! We have nothing like it in Japan.'

Watercolour of Sidney Smirke's planned Orangery at Gunnersbury, post 1843

The turn of the twentieth century brought a new generation of horticulturalists to the fore. Lionel grew up during a time of radical change in gardening and, with his family background, he was ideally placed to learn about new concepts. In August 1906, the *Third International Conference* took place in London, on genetics: it was the first occasion on which the term 'genetics' had been used. The RHS had approached Leo for support and it was apparent that, with his many European connections, he did much to encourage international delegates to attend. Unfortunately, Leo himself was unable to join the conference as he was away in Switzerland. Instead it was Lionel, aged 24, who listened attentively to the hybridisation conference proceedings, doubtless storing up this knowledge for the future.

The vote of thanks of the conference delegates following lunch at Gunnersbury House and tour of Gunnersbury Park in the afternoon was warm indeed: 'What is even more valued, however, is such a courteous and kindly reception and welcome of Britishers and foreigners alike in one of our great English homes, and the opportunity of seeing its most beautiful gardens – surpassing even those of Damascus – its artistic treasures, and its princely hospitality.'

The treasures of Gunnersbury were not always confined there. As mentioned above, the great gardening event of 1912 was the Royal International Horticultural Exhibition in the grounds of the Royal Hospital, Chelsea. This was the first international exhibition since 1866, when it was held on a smaller scale in South Kensington. Crowds – more than 200,000 people over eight days – flocked to see the displays of horticulture on show in the exhibition tents, the main one being the largest ever erected to date, at 660 ft long and 45 ft high, covering three-and-a-half acres of ground and lit by electricity. The enormous exhibit submitted by Leo took centre stage at the show, occupying 1,380 square feet. A score of vans was required to transport the fruit trees that were part of the stunning display from Gunnersbury to the show ground.

Like his father, Lionel learnt a huge amount from the Gunnersbury head gardeners, respecting and trusting their skill and horticultural knowledge.

Hudson served Gunnersbury for 27 years. On his retirement, he said his purpose was to have 'endeavoured to carry out three principles – to serve his employer to the best of his ability, to further the work they had started, and to assist those of the craft who needed assistance'. Lionel would bring first Fred Kneller (1868–1926) from Gunnersbury Park and then Hudson's successor, Arthur Bedford (1874–1934), with him to advise on his future gardens, including Exbury, which was to involve a transformation even more extraordinary than that of Gunnersbury.

above · Blue water lily (*N. nouchali var. caerulea*)

below · The staff, Gunnersbury Park

GUNNERSBURY PARK.
NOVEMBER, 1914.

Lionel before Exbury

LIFE IN THE FAST LANE

CHAPTER 2

The years before his purchase of Exbury were far from idle ones for Lionel de Rothschild.

After attending Harrow School and Trinity College, Cambridge, Lionel's formal entry into society took the form of an elaborate 21st birthday party at Ascott House in January 1903, held jointly with his cousin, Harry Primrose (1882–1974), whose parents were Archibald Primrose, 5th Earl of Rosebery (1847–1929) and his wife, Hannah, née de Rothschild (1851–1890).

The evening reception featured his uncle Alfred de Rothschild's private orchestra from his Buckinghamshire residence, Halton House. However, the term 'orchestra' may be a touch misleading; family lore has it that the musical ability of the players was less important than their appearance: they all had to be the same height and sport a moustache.

A tenants' ball was held on the cricket grounds in a huge tent elaborately decorated with carpets, mirrors and floral arrangements provided by Mr Jennings, Ascott's head gardener. Among numerous toasts and presentations, a beautifully illustrated testimonial was given to Lionel by the tradesmen serving the Ascott estate. Mr Jennings' contribution was another reminder of the gardening inheritance that would inspire Lionel's extraordinary achievements at Exbury. And yet gardening was not Lionel's only passion.

Like a number of his contemporaries, Lionel devoted much of his spare time to fast cars and boats. Cars had been a feature of Britain's roads since the end of the nineteenth century and motoring became a passion that Lionel took to with characteristic energy. His father Leopold had bought one of the first cars in England and shared his interest with his friend the Prince of Wales, later King Edward VII, whose endorsement made cars popular with the titled and wealthy. Driving was then viewed as a sport rather than the mundane mode of transport it eventually – to some extent – was to become.

Lionel with friends at the wheel of one of his cars *previous pages · see page 197*

25TH JANUARY, 1903.

TO Lionel De Rothschild Esq.,

ASCOTT, LEIGHTON BUZZARD.

SIR

WE, the undersigned, having business relations with Ascott, beg to offer you our respectful and heartfelt congratulations on the attainment of your Majority. IT is our sincerest wish that you and all dear to you may enjoy a long life of perfect happiness and contentment. WE earnestly hope that you may long continue to reside amongst us, that you may follow in the footsteps of your honored and beloved Parents, and of your illustrious Grandfather whose name you bear; and that you may worthily maintain the traditions of your Family which has endeared itself to the hearts of all by its noble qualities and its generous sympathy with every good cause.

CONCORDIA · INTEGRITAS · INDUSTRIA

STET · FORTUNA · DOMUS

VIRTUS · VERA · NOBILITAS

Abbott, Thomas	Fortnum S.	Mallett, T.	Robinson, James
Abraham, Mark	Foster, Henry	Mayne & Sons,	Ruggles, C.F.
Arnold, Joseph	Garside, George	Meager, John	Scrivener & Son
Aveline &	Gibbs & Co,	Morgan & Co,	Smyth, H.G.
D'Phillips,	Grace Fresh	Oates, W.W.	Spiers, J.
Bardell, W.	Haskins, John	Osgood, Walter	Tattam, Edward
Bentley, Joseph	Heady, Joseph	Page, Arthur	Taylor, Fresh
Brown George	Hear, Thomas	Page, George	Towers, WY
& Sons,	Inns, A.C.	Page, William	Tustin, Martin J.
Brown, H.G.	Inns, F.W.	Paul & Son	Veitch & Sons,
Canning, Philip	Jackson, H.	Payne, S.G.	Waterer Anthony
Cutbush & Son	Lane & Sons,	Pollard, MY.A.S.	Webster &
Dickson &	Lehmann MY.	Purrett, R.	Cannon,
Robinson,	Mackrill, E.T. &	Reader, John	Willard, MY
Durrell, W.S.	Sons,		Wilson, James
Eady & Dulley,			Wood & Co,
Field & Son,			Yirrell, Thomas
			Richardson, Chas

1882   1903

Angel Studio, London

It was not that sporty at first, however: the Locomotive Act of 1865, known as the 'Red Flag Act', had required a person carrying a red flag to walk at least 60 yards ahead of any self-propelled vehicle, imposed speed limits of 4 mph in the country, 2 mph in town and a £10 fine for speeding. Its repeal in 1896 scrapped the flag and raised the speed limit to 14 mph. Those who could afford the luxury of a motor car now began to enjoy higher speeds without being apprehended by an – inevitably – breathless policeman.

Lionel's early favourite was an Orleans, built at the Orleans Works in Twickenham but based on the Belgian Vivinus car; he owned many other smart cars, including Rolls-Royces, Mercedes, Napiers, Wolseleys and Siddeleys. He went on motoring tours of Europe and North Africa, taking his own mechanic, Martin Harper. Later his cars were customised: the bodywork was blue with a yellow coachline and the interior also had dark blue leather.

Other Rothschilds joined in the driving craze and stiff family competition arose. The Coupe Rothschild, awarded to the winner of a motor race in Nice, was given by Lionel's French cousin, Henri de Rothschild (1872–1947), whom Lionel, aged 23, beat in an 18-hour race from Paris to Monte Carlo. Lionel and his brother Anthony (1887–1961) were members of the Cambridge University Automobile Club. It is reasonable to suggest that Lionel may not have had a perfect road safety record – though one of his driving mishaps was so bizarre that 'road safety' may not be the right term. *The Times* reported in March 1907 that a motoring accident had occurred with Lionel sustaining superficial cuts about the face when the goggles he was wearing 'came into violent contact with the head of a horse attached to a milk float'.

Fast boats were another interest. John Douglas-Scott-Montagu (1866–1929), later 2nd Lord Montagu, was a great friend of Lionel and shared his passion for speed on the water. They spent many weekends trialling their boats on the Solent, culminating in the summer Cowes Week on the Isle of Wight. They were equally successful abroad, winning the Harmsworth Trophy, the first annual international award for motorboat racing, with their racing boat *Napier II* in 1905; in 1906 they broke the world water speed record – at the then staggering speed of 28.8 knots – and the next year they won the *Perla del Mediterraneo*. These times spent with Montagu in the surroundings of the Hampshire coastline undoubtedly drew Lionel closer to the area where he would eventually reside and embark upon his greatest achievement.

39

opposite
Twenty-first birthday greetings to Lionel from businesses local to Ascott, with vignettes showing scenes from his education and leisure

top
Lionel on the campaign trail with Mariloo

above
The *Perla del Mediterraneo*, an enamelled plaque by René Lalique

Lionel's autochromes taken on honeymoon showing the
Colosseum (*top*) and Mariloo in the Forum, Rome (*opposite*)
and the harbour by Villa Kérylos, Beaulieu-sur-Mer (*above*)

above
Lionel and Mariloo in the south of
France some years after their honeymoon

But there was more to the younger Lionel than fast cars and
boats. Contribution to public service and British political affairs
ran in the family. Lionel's grandfather, after whom he was
named, had become the first Jewish Member of Parliament in
1847. However, it took 11 years of political wrangling to overturn
the bar to a non-Christian joining the House of Commons: he
eventually took his seat in 1858, a victory for adherents of all
faiths. His son Natty became MP for Aylesbury in 1865 and was
given a peerage as Lord Rothschild of Tring in 1885 – the first
Jewish member of the House of Lords. Ferdinand de Rothschild

(1839–1898) followed as the Liberal MP for Aylesbury and, after
his death, Walter Rothschild (1868–1937) was elected unopposed
for the Liberal Unionists. Lionel was the next member of his
family to represent the area; he was chosen as the MP for
Aylesbury in 1910. He spoke in the House of Commons on key
issues both for his constituents and for the Jewish community
and dutifully served his constituency until 1923.

Marriage came to Lionel relatively late – at least for the time. He
was 30 when he married Marie-Louise Beer ('Mariloo'), to whom
he had been introduced by Robert de Rothschild (1880–1946).

Lionel before Exbury · Life in the fast lane

Inchmery House, which had been modelled on a seaside villa, with a wide veranda, large gardens and access straight onto the beach below, was perfect for someone who loved both the sea and gardening.

A grandson of the founder of the French branch of the bank, de Rothschild Frères, Robert had married Gabrielle ('Nelly') (1886–1945), the elder sister of Mariloo in 1907, thus leading to the introduction.

Due to the untimely death earlier that month of Mariloo's father, the couple had a quiet, private marriage ceremony in October 1912, on the small family estate at St Germain, just outside Paris. Their honeymoon began at Fontainebleau, followed by a driving tour around Europe taking in the Italian lakes and gardens.

One more of Lionel's interests was autochrome photography – he was a talented photographer – and he took numerous pictures of the scenery. He took quite a few of his new wife too, giving Mariloo more than a hint of the stoicism his enthusiasms would require of her, photography being a somewhat lengthy procedure in those days. Mariloo, however, showed characteristic patience. That said, her oldest granddaughter once asked her what her honeymoon was like. 'Oh it was alright,' she replied, without great enthusiasm. 'Your grandfather planned the menus for the next two years.'

Freshly married and looking for a new country residence for his family, Lionel focused on the beautiful Hampshire countryside near to the estate of his friend John Montagu at Beaulieu in the New Forest. It was the adjoining Exbury estate that drew his attention: to view the house and gardens he drove down from London past Southampton towards Hythe and Fawley, where the scenery changed and the wilds of the New Forest appeared as a flat and rough landscape dotted with New Forest ponies. He turned off the road to Beaulieu and drove through the woodlands along Summer Lane to Exbury village. Once there, he breathed in the air of the place that would define his whole life.

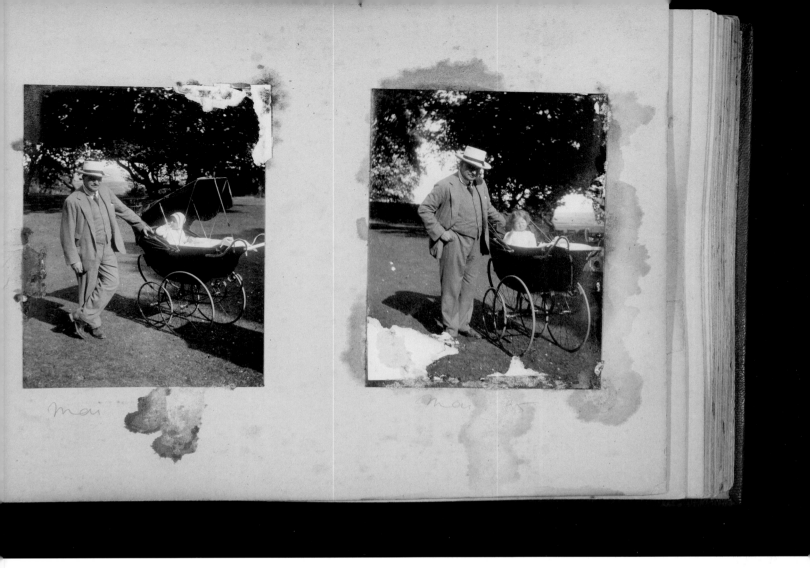

opposite and above · Photographs from Mariloo's album, showing life at Inchmery with their children, Rosemary and Eddy

The Exbury estate, however, was not for sale, but he found a nearby property overlooking the Solent: Inchmery House. The couple settled into Inchmery House in 1912, while spending the working week at their London house off Park Lane. Mariloo never lost her French accent and, though initially a little shy, she soon embraced her new role in the rural community. Her quiet nature complemented the boundless energy of her single-minded husband. In 1913, she gave birth to their first child, Rosemary.

Ever industrious with his gardening, Lionel moved many of his plants from Gunnersbury to Inchmery and, as he accumulated more, additional space was needed to show them off in their full glory. He planned a transformation of Inchmery, laying out an elaborate garden, with an intention to rebuild the house round a courtyard and to make a new driveway. Ironically, these big ideas were stalled by a relatively small obstacle: a post box stood in the way of Lionel's plans and permission to move it halted progress.

In any event, there were soon more pressing issues to worry about as conflict in Europe threatened the peace and tranquillity of the countryside. On 4 August 1914, war was declared.

above
Rosemary and Eddy on the
foreshore overlooking the Solent
and the Isle of Wight, painted by
Sir Alfred Munnings, 1923

opposite
Rosemary and Eddy (*centre*) with
friends. Children of neighbouring
families often feature in Mariloo's
photograph albums

Chapter Two

below
Lionel in the dress uniform of
the Buckinghamshire Yeomanry
(Royal Bucks Hussars); he was
appointed a captain in August 1910

right
Looking into the courtyard at
New Court from the Partners'
Entrance. Lionel's grandfather,
father and sons would also have
known this view

opposite
St. Katharine's Church, Exbury

N M Rothschild & Sons was seen at the time as a financial institution of great importance in which Lionel and his two brothers already played a role. To ensure its continuity, it was felt that there must be a young Rothschild kept safely at New Court as Lionel's father, Leo, and his two uncles, Alfred and Natty, were now old men. Lionel and his two brothers had joined the family's traditional regiment, the Buckinghamshire Yeomanry (the Royal Bucks Hussars). Lionel's brothers, Evelyn and Anthony, went off to war but Lionel – requested by the King himself – had reluctantly to stay behind; he felt frustrated and there is no doubt it affected him. Still, politics and enlistment were issues where he could contribute to the war effort. New Court was transformed into a recruitment centre at which, dressed in his uniform, he encouraged men to sign up. As a serving MP he spoke up in the House of Commons on behalf of the Jewish Recruiting Committee of the East End of London and in December 1917 he was appointed Parliamentary Private Secretary to the Ministry of National Service.

The bank was prepared for war. The gallery in the Dividend Office was sandbagged to protect the Bullion Room underneath. Departments were moved around to reduce disruption to daily business. In 1917 the daylight raids began and Lionel's uncle Alfred, who was of a nervous disposition, had a shelter constructed in the Drawn Bond department.

News came in November 1917 of the tragic death of Evelyn from wounds sustained in a cavalry charge against the Turks at El Mughar, Palestine. At home, more tragedies struck as the older members of the family did indeed die off and Lionel's responsibilities were to increase over the last year of the war: Leopold died in May 1917, followed in January 1918 by Alfred; Natty had predeceased them in 1915. Anthony survived the war years. He fought at Gallipoli and was mentioned in dispatches, returning wounded to serve in France until the end of the war.

Leopold's widow Marie continued to live at Gunnersbury after his death, reducing the staff and settling into widowhood. Alfred had bequeathed Halton House, his house in Buckinghamshire, to Lionel together with its collection of pictures, porcelain and furniture. He had also had an illegitimate daughter, Almina Wombwell (1876–1969), who became the Countess of Carnarvon by marriage in 1895. She received his townhouse, Seamore Place, and its contents. Some of this money funded the 1922 expedition of Almina's husband, Lord Carnarvon (1866–1923), to the Valley of the Kings and the discovery of the tomb of Tutankhamun by Howard Carter (1874–1939).

The clay soil of the Chiltern Hills and its location had no attraction for Lionel. Halton House had been occupied by the Royal Flying Corps during the war and it was a long way from Inchmery, where his family was expanding with the arrival of young Edmund in 1916, soon to be followed by Naomi in 1920. In 1918 he sold Halton to the Air Ministry for £112,000 – as a patriotic gesture, well below probate – and took the contents with him. At that moment the opportunity arose to buy Exbury.

Harry Forster (1866–1936) had inherited the Exbury estate from his father in 1886 and married Rachel Douglas-Scott-Montagu (1868–1962), daughter of Henry, 1st Baron Montagu (1832–1905) in 1890. As a young man he had played cricket for Oxford and Hampshire; Forster was also a keen yachtsman, a Conservative MP and served in the War Office during the First World War. He had moved to the adjoining property of Lepe, along the seashore from Inchmery, and had let Exbury House out to tenants; in 1919 he was elevated to the peerage, becoming Baron Forster of Lepe. Tragically, Forster's sons John (1893–1914) and Alfred (1898–1919) were killed in the war, the former less than two months from its start and the latter dying of wounds sustained mere weeks from its end. A beautiful bronze statue of Alfred in uniform lies in their honour in Exbury church. Forster was offered the role of Governor-General of Australia (1920–25), which he readily took; he now had no male heirs and rather than continue to let Exbury House, he sold it outright to Lionel in 1919.

47

Exbury before Lionel

'An earthly paradise'

CHAPTER 3

Beaulieu Woods, from Saltern Grove Exbury

View showing the Beaulieu
River from the Exbury side,
from drawings and paintings by
Philadelphia Mitford in the late
eighteenth century

previous pages · see page 197

Long before the Forsters arrived, Exbury had been shaped by a lengthy history of different family ownership. Settlements have been recorded there from the Iron Age to its appearance in the Domesday Book in 1086 as 'Teocreberie'. The Foliat family acquired the village in the thirteenth century and later a substantial manor and church was built for John de Bettesthorne (1329–1399) who settled there in the early fourteenth century. Through marriage in the fifteenth century the Berkeley family inherited the manor until it descended through the wider family to the Comptons of Compton Wynyates, Warwickshire, who held it for the next 200 years.

The first of a long line of Mitford ownership occurred in 1718, when the merchant William Mitford (c.1673–1747) and his wife Margaret Edwards (c.1689–1720) acquired land at Exbury; he had already bought the Newtown estate near Lymington in 1711 and owned Gilbury House, adjoining Exbury. He developed the grounds further, laying out formal groves with woodland beyond; he planted cedars, including a Cedar of Lebanon planted in 1729 that still grows at the end of the Glade today. While its date is uncertain, it seems likely that one of the eighteenth century Mitfords was responsible for another iconic tree, the *Platanus orientalis* that lies a bit beyond the Glade. The old central part remains upright but this tree has the ability to layer itself and two gigantic limbs, whether from layers or suckers, snake out to either side, with further ones elsewhere in the bushes. Not surprisingly, it is known at Exbury as the 'Wiggly Tree'. Other examples grace several Oxbridge colleges and, most notably, a fine circle is to be found at Blickling in Norfolk. William died in 1747 and his son John Mitford (1712–1761), and John's wife

Philadelphia Reveley (1721–1797), inherited the estate. In turn his son William Mitford (1744–1827), and his wife Frances Molloy (1745–1776), then came into the estate, and it was he who built an impressive new house looking across to the Isle of Wight. Today's Exbury used to be known as Upper Exbury, until the church was moved there in 1827, at which point the original settlement by the river mouth became known as Lower Exbury. Inside the present church there remains a tablet on the north wall with the Mitford boar's head and family motto 'God caryth for us'.

This Mitford was MP for a number of constituencies between 1785 and 1818. He was also a well-read Greek scholar: encouraged by his fellow South Hampshire Militiaman and author, Edward Gibbon (1737–1794), he published his own work, *The History of Greece*, in 1784.

It was Mitford who first undertook significant landscaping at Exbury: he established distinctive rides circling the estate and 'cross walks' for visitors to enjoy the 'grand river-views' through the trees to the Beaulieu River and across the Solent to the Isle of Wight. Mitford – known as 'the old Colonel' – was remembered by his great-grandson as being 'a very skilful forester and gardener. I possess an old, much worn pruning knife with a horn handle which he always carried about when he was engaged in his favourite pursuit of landscape gardening.'

Exbury was praised by William Gilpin (1724–1804), the eighteenth-century pioneer of the picturesque movement and a key influence on the 'high phase' of landscape style. He advocated – with some force – that his disciples move away from the man-made naturalness of Capability Brown in which he found the artificial lakes, temples and views not to his taste

('awkward and disgusting') and encouraged them to embrace the 'unfettered' scenery on their doorstep. Jane Austen (1775–1817), who lived further north in Hampshire, in Chawton, echoed these sentiments in *Pride and Prejudice*, where Elizabeth is delighted by her first view of Pemberley: 'She had never seen a place for which nature had done more, or where natural beauty had been so little counteracted by an awkward taste.' A former teacher of Mitford, Gilpin passed through Hampshire on his Western Tour in 1775 and visited the Mitfords' estate at Exbury, a visit later documented in his publication *Remarks on Forest Scenery* (1791). He reported that, '[T]he house is no object: but the scenery consists of a more beautiful profusion of wood, water and varied grounds, than is commonly to be met with.'

He admired the picturesque qualities of Exbury's groves and woodlands where Mitford had cleared his grandfather's formal *allées* and created the groups of trees that Gilpin found so attractive. 'We had everywhere instances of the beauty of the trees as *individuals* – as uniting in *clumps* – and as spreading into *woods*; for all here is pure nature: and as they were beginning now to put on their autumnal attire, we were entertained with the beauties of *colouring* as well as *form*.' He celebrated the lack of ornament at Exbury – a sideways swipe at the temple-filled landscapes of Capability Brown.

53

these and following pages
Postcards and photographs
of village life by New Forest
photographer Edward Mudge

Bucklers Hard & Exbury Point; from the dark wood.

'There is scarce a gravel-walk made: no pavilion raised; nor even a white-seat fixed. And yet in fact, more is done, than if all these decorations, and a hundred others, had been added, unaccompanied with what has been done.'

Mitford later offered Gilpin the position of vicar of nearby Boldre, a post to which Gilpin devoted himself, building a poor-house and school and working tirelessly for his parishioners until his death in 1804.

above
View of the Beaulieu River by Philadelphia Mitford

opposite
View across to the shipyard at Buckler's Hard by Philadelphia Mitford

The proximity of the sea and the Beaulieu River brought the brickmaking and shipbuilding trades to Gilbury and Exbury. In the late eighteenth century naval ships were built from New Forest timber at Buckler's Hard and fought in the Napoleonic wars, notably HMS *Agamemnon*, HMS *Euryalus* and HMS *Swiftsure*. Nelson captained the *Agamemnon* from 1793–1796 and all three ships fought at the Battle of Trafalgar; indeed an earlier HMS *Swiftsure* had been captured by the French and fought on their side at Trafalgar but was recaptured.

Mitford died peacefully in his sleep at Exbury in 1827 and his grandson, Henry Reveley Mitford (1804–1883), husband of Lady Georgina Ashburnham Mitford (1805–1882), inherited the estate, his father having died in the wreck of his ship in 1803. He was a magistrate and Deputy Lieutenant of the county. One of his improvements to the garden, around 1868, was a ha-ha in front of the house to separate the fields or 'Park' from the formal lawn.

In his *Memories*, his son Algernon 'Barty' Freeman Mitford, 1st Baron Redesdale (1837–1916), recounted an unusual incident that befell him on a lone visit to the house. After retiring to bed following a solitary dinner (and, it should be added, 'a pint of claret') he was awakened by 'a most uncanny noise in the room over my head'. He heard the dragging of a heavy weight in the room over his head and then down the stairs 'bump, bump, bump' to his bedroom door and 'then there was silence for a minute or two, and presently the weight was dragged up again … and all was still'. On his return to London, he told his father who, 'a good deal startled', told him that one of his grandfather's (Algernon's great-grandfather's) 'eccentricities' had been to pull a heavy trunk around an upstairs room for exercise after 'a long day's literary work'.

Algernon Mitford would go on to purchase Batsford Park in the Cotswolds, where he created a fine arboretum. In the 1880s Reveley Mitford sold Exbury to John Forster (1826–1886), a man with 'a natural gift of manner and attractive graciousness', bringing to an end the time of the Mitfords at Exbury. Algernon, called it 'an earthly paradise', and so it was to remain.

'Banker by hobby…
gardener by profession'

LIONEL AT EXBURY, 1919–1929

CHAPTER 4

Exbury became Lionel's
in April 1919: Exbury House,
2,600 acres of land, several
farms and the tiny hamlet
of Exbury were acquired for
a total of £60,000.

opposite · Home Wood   above · Exbury House at the time of Lionel's purchase, showing the magnolia he was keen to preserve   previous pages · see page 197

On a warm spring day Lionel introduced his wife, Mariloo, to the garden. Standing by her side on a lawn studded with weeds, he spoke of his vision: 'The charm about this place lies in its surroundings ... what a wonderful scope for a rhododendron wood.' Grabbing a couple of billhooks, the couple made their way through the jungle of scrub and sycamore saplings to look for the cypress trees that had been planted by a young Algernon Mitford many years before.

As a boy at Eton, Mitford had witnessed the grand funeral procession of the Duke of Wellington in London, noting, 'all men doffed their hats as if he had been a king.' A wreath of hallowed cypress fell off the heavily laden funeral car and an old woman 'dashed forward and picked up the wreath', whereupon Mitford endeavoured to buy it from her. She would not give up 'her precious relic' easily but – in exchange for a shilling – she parted with one cypress cone, which Mitford sent down to the gardeners at Exbury.

Lionel intended to remodel the Mitfords' 'rather derelict mansion' and chose his architects carefully. He engaged Romaine-Walker and Jenkins, a London firm familiar with the demands of their clientele and one that could be trusted to handle the transformation of Exbury House into the type of house he wanted: he aimed to refashion it in a neoclassical style, reminiscent of his childhood home of Gunnersbury.

The original Mitford house was rather unusual: a triangle with a large circular hall at its centre gave, as Mitford explained in his notes, morning sun in his dining room and evening sun in the drawing room but shade in the library. The nineteenth century had seen this reshaped to a smaller version of what is there today. Lionel added an ionic colonnade with a central bow on the front, the old house being considerably enlarged and faced with honey-coloured Bath stone. On the west side of the house, a specimen of *Magnolia grandiflora* was carefully preserved.

Lionel wanted the balance of modern living with the decorative qualities of the houses he had grown up in: thus the interior displayed some of the lovely seventeenth-century Dutch landscapes and eighteenth-century French and English portraits from Halton House. It appears, however, that he did not like being disturbed and in contrast to the comfort and elegance, the only telephone in the house was in a tiny room below stairs.

Having decided on the look of the house, Lionel set about making his garden. He took the advice of P.D. Williams (1865–1935) and J.C. Williams (1861–1939), two cousins whom he referred to as 'his gardening godfathers'; they had already

61

Exbury House being enlarged for Lionel and Mariloo

established wonderful woodland gardens in Cornwall, P.D. at Lanarth and J.C. at Caerhays. He heeded their practical advice to 'plant your shelter first ... before attempting to build up your garden' and then to cut down undergrowth and trees to leave drifts between which to plant his rhododendrons and azaleas.

By the end of the first year ten acres had been cleared around Home Wood, which runs from the house down towards the river. Lionel planted hardier hybrids on the exposed edges and then some of the more tender (or 'choicer') hybrids and plants in the sheltered areas. For the next ten years he was to employ up to 150 men from miles around just to prepare the soil; they were known as the 'trenching team'. They double-dug the soil

'two spits deep' and where the soil was gravelly, mixed in 'a little peaty leaf soil' from the neighbouring woods to create a perfect base for Lionel's acid-loving plants; in all cases a little was put around the rhododendrons and azaleas when planted. In places he also mulched in spent hops, a memorable smell for those who worked there.

By 1920 Lionel had made something of a name for himself as a rhododendron grower. In September of that year, as a newly-invited member, he reported on the conditions in the garden to the Rhododendron Society. He praised the temperate climate at Exbury, which benefited from the warm air of the Gulf Stream arriving from the Solent. Lack of water, however, was a

clockwise from top · Construction of the sawmill in the Estate Yard; R.'Loderi Game Chick'; cascades below Top Pond

big concern ('drought is my worst enemy'). He once described driving from Southampton to Exbury in the pouring rain, looking to the thundery Isle of Wight – while Exbury was as dry as a bone.

There were a couple of good springs in the woods and the water was acid, so vital for ericaceous plants, but Lionel needed more: it is said he paid for a dowser to come all the way from London to look for water, to the amusement of the locals who reckoned he could have got the local dowser to do it for free. Once he had sunk his boreholes, he laid an elaborate network of irrigation pipes – some 22 miles in all – and built a new water tower over the estate office, primarily for all his greenhouses. In all, 26 miles of path were laid over the hidden pipes to keep them root-free and accessible; the path was also wide enough for Lionel to drive his car. As a Director of the Armstrong Siddeley motor company, he had requested a 'small run-around' to use in the gardens: he reported back, 'I love the little 10hp Siddeley I have at Exbury.'

As he did not yet have his own hybrids, he had to plant other people's, which he sourced chiefly from the trade, his Cornish friends and the collection of Sir Edmund Loder of Leonardslee in Sussex. Although many were later replaced by his own plants, looking back in an article he wrote in 1940, he gives them their due. Thus at the beginning of the Glade he placed a bank of R.'Christmas Cheer' – as its name suggests, the earliest to flower.

The building team and craftsmen supervised by the clerk of works, Mr Johnson

On the south side of the Glade he put among other things some pink R. arboreum, R. 'Boddaertianum', the pure white R. 'Helene Schiffner', the bright red R. 'Gill's Crimson' and R. 'Mrs P.D. Williams', with its browny yellow eye. Along the sunnier north side he had to put hardier plants, including some Knap Hill hybrids from Waterers (a regular supplier of the Rothschild family whose influence was to increase greatly in the coming years): R. 'Purple Splendour', R. 'Lady Clementine Mitford' and, ensuring both gardening godfathers were happy, R. 'Mrs J.C. Williams'. No garden is ever static; some of this planting has changed since Lionel's day and some remains. The hybrids from Leonardslee were of course from the

famous R. Loderi Group, notably R. 'Loderi King George' and the original plant of R. 'Loderi Venus'; these opulent rhododendrons still stand, scenting the air with their fragrance at the height of the season.

Although no sketches or drawings survive to reveal how Lionel's mind mapped out his garden, it is possible to see that he did not fight with nature but sought to use the features already within the landscape and adapt them to meet his need to create shade, shelter, and vistas where the plants and the surrounding landscape complemented each other.

He continued to pursue this vision at the Top, Middle and Bottom Ponds in Home Wood and the pretty cascades – now

Boudoir 1924

above · Interior shot; Lionel and Mariloo with guests

planted with hostas, rodgersia and maples – running between them. Here, head gardener Fred Kneller oversaw the installation of concrete pond linings and dams. An island in the middle of Top Pond was planted with a splendid *Taxodium distichum*; after the war the late-flowering R.'Purple Emperor' was put at its base, complementing some fiery orange azaleas. Generally Lionel did not think rhododendrons and azaleas mixed well together but thought azaleas looked good either on their own or against the dark green of rhododendrons that had flowered earlier in the year. He placed a large edging of Kurume azaleas by the Middle Pond and further down, a drift of R.'Hinomayo' – in Lionel's opinion the hardiest and best pink of all of the Kurumes – was placed in front of a big group of earlier flowering big-leaved rhododendrons. Around the Bottom Pond he grouped more Kurume azaleas which he ordered in 1920 directly from the Yokohoma Nursery in Japan, asking for 30 of the so-called 'Wilson Fifty' (50 Kurume azaleas selected by the plant hunter Ernest Wilson of the Arnold Arboretum). This sort of landscaping, in a layered tapestry, was Lionel's vision and unlike anything then found in Japan. There azaleas were grown in container cultivation; Lionel released them. This approach was later copied in the Punchbowl in The Valley Garden, Windsor and at Exbury after the war in the Wynniatt bowl round the Middle Pond.

While gradually he introduced more and more of his own hybrids, he also used older ones, like a large group of R. 'Loder's White' or a drift of R. 'Queen Wilhelmina'; while some of his planting is gone, both these groups are still there. New hybrids by other people also found a place, like the pretty Waterer hybrid R. 'Mrs Lionel de Rothschild' and the early-flowering R. 'Choremia' from Bodnant. He liked to plant in big groups – after all, he had the room – and given the relatively flat nature of the landscape, liked to present the walker with a surprise effect as he or she came round a corner, and then not repeat that effect. Some plants naturally worked better in groups, like the large purple R. augustinii: he bred within the species to intensify the colour and made a walk of them to the east of Home Wood and later planted a glorious mass of them at the other end of the garden at Augustinii Corner. A Japanese bridge, referencing the one at Monet's garden at Giverny, was added to cross where the stream from St. Mary's Spring entered the Top Pond. The bench looking down to it from where the spring issues has always been known as 'Mrs Lionel's seat'. In a nice touch, this is now surrounded by the rhododendrons Lionel bred that are named after her and their four children.

For woodland colour, Lionel followed what he saw as William Robinson's philosophy, writing, 'The real art of gardening is not only to group plants to make a picture but also to see that colours mingle well. What has been done in herbaceous borders can just as well be done on a large scale in the woodland with azaleas and rhododendrons.' With this in mind, he constantly tinkered with colour combinations to avoid clashes – too many gardens, he felt, had been 'planted with no eye to colour'. He himself had no compunction in moving things around – their 'little walks' – even in flower; while they were still small this was not difficult but if they were too large, 'the axe should be frequently used'.

below and opposite · The Japanese bridge and Top Pond in autumn and winter

By 1923 the gardens were rapidly transforming, sustained by the propagation of seeds and plants from plant hunters, botanic gardens and fellow enthusiasts that kept arriving at the two-acre estate yard. There were 60 trained gardening staff plus 15 in the glasshouses, all of them ably led by Arthur Bedford. When the hundreds of packets of seed arrived, the range and variety were a challenge. Even for experienced gardeners, it was a task to get unknown seeds to grow; they often had to rely on handwritten labels, field notes and sketches for clues. Mr Bedford kept a watchful eye over the progress of these precious charges.

Indoors, the gardeners were also busy layering, grafting, budding or propagating by division or by root cuttings, while those outside were equally busy planting thousands of trees, evergreen and deciduous shrubs, bulbs, herbaceous perennials and annuals, which Lionel purchased in vast quantities from nurseries far and wide. The exchange of seed with universities, arboretums and collections from around the world added further complexity to an already demanding workload.

Lionel recorded everything in meticulous detail. He kept card indexes for the rhododendron species, hybrids and specimen trees; he noted where they were planted and often exactly when they flowered each year. He scrawled notes: thus by *Magnolia stellata* he wrote, 'An attractive picture is made by planting this shrub in a group growing beneath it thickly grape hyacinths (blue). The two flower together.' In Lionel's stud book his crosses took sequential 'LR' numbers; initially the thought was for the names to follow the years alphabetically, but this was soon abandoned. He would eventually record 1,210 hybrids, of which over a third were named and registered with the RHS, and wrote, 'I think I have obtained more pleasure in the last twenty years from seeing my own hybrids grow and flower – in spite of the fact that many have been failures – than from any other form of gardening.'

The glasshouses at Exbury were colourful all year long. Replacing the Victorian bedding, geraniums and carnations familiar to Lionel from his youth were more orchids, clivias, hippeastrums, nerines and tender rhododendrons neatly lined up in the complex of glasshouses, cold frames and vineries. The vibrant cut blooms lit up the dinner table and corridors and baskets of vegetables, fruit and flowers would also be sent up to the London house.

Lionel did not want an 'architectural hothouse' like the huge winter garden-style orangery at Halton, or the elegant fruit-filled Gunnersbury orangery. He used his glasshouses for purely horticultural purposes, hybridisation and growing on – experimentation on a huge scale. MacKenzie Moncur Ltd. was commissioned to design teak glasshouses requiring some 60,000 square feet of glass and a specialised Rhododendron House; in a nice example of recycling, it has always been said that the teak came from decommissioned tea clippers. MacKenzie Moncur's clients and projects included the King, Edward VII, who commissioned the company to rebuild the glasshouses at Windsor in 1905, the Palm House in Sefton Park, Liverpool, and the north and south blocks of the Temperate House at Kew.

The four clear-span orchid houses were 170 feet long, each set against a three-quarter-span vinery with a purpose-built laboratory to one side and the head gardener's office to the other. The outline designs of the clear-span Rhododendron House were drawn up in March 1925. The proposed structure on a north-south axis was over 119 feet long and 54 feet wide, and the top ridge reached nearly 38 feet high. It had two tiers of glass with a central bell-like top section.

Lionel eventually decided on a much simpler approach, getting his own team to construct and erect the new house for his tender rhododendrons. Houses for figs, grapes and peaches leant against the walls of the kitchen garden. The boilers next to the Fig House powered the glasshouse heating and ensured a constant temperature, essential in the winter, and the whole range of greenhouses was flanked by a herbaceous border 140 yards long.

His arrival as owner of the estate led to immense changes in Exbury village, a close-knit community of charming cottages, gravel roads, a school and St. Katharine's Church. Lionel began an extensive building programme in the village: new houses were needed to accommodate the staff and the large number of workers that arrived to work in the gardens. These 'New Cottages' were built from red brick with tiled roofs and oak windows in a pseudo-Arts and Crafts style. They were extremely modern, with a water tap inside, an indoor toilet and a bathroom. Electricity came later. A laundry was built opposite the nineteenth-century gatehouses to service the big house. A new Bothy was constructed for the unmarried gardeners and accommodation for the house staff was integrated into the remodelled Exbury House.

Lionel gave the village a clubhouse on the recreation ground with a cricket pitch, tennis courts and football field. Most of the villagers worked for the estate and this was where everyone gathered on the weekend. There was no pub in Exbury, so it was the only place where alcohol was served. Saturday night get-togethers were accompanied by the village dance band and billiards, and there was a lively annual children's party.

Craftsmen – bricklayers, carpenters, plumbers and joiners – were brought in, eager for work after the war, to be managed by the clerk of works Mr Johnson (1880–1951). They stayed in the village and at the nearby Blacklands Farm while working in the new estate yard where the blacksmith made the steel girders and men in the sawmill cut the timber for the glasshouses. Building materials were initially delivered by a steam traction engine

above and right
The village began to thrive under Lionel's care: New Cottages and a village cricket team from later years

opposite
Naomi, Rosemary with Leo, Eddy and their cousin Renée on the balcony at Exbury House; Eddy in his toy plane and a greetings card showing the three eldest children

from the train at Beaulieu Road station, eight miles away. This may have contributed to the eventual collapse of the bridge at Beaulieu; in any case, the traction engine was replaced by a steady stream of lorries. The village-shop-cum-post-office supplied essentials and the local farm offered fresh milk. Enthusiastic vegetable growing kept estate workers healthy (as did the fruit trees) and led to fierce competition at the annual village flower show. This was the highlight of the year, a grand affair opened (and paid for) by Lionel and Mariloo.

There were also cricket matches against local teams and the enthusiastically contested tug of war. Lionel always made a speech and noted sadly in 1939 that he doubted whether they would ever happen again. Nevertheless, though much diminished in scale, such events did continue. In fact, on one memorable occasion Exbury won the tug of war against the much stronger Cadland team – through the simple expedient of the Inchmery gardener, George Nicholas (1916–77) tying his end of the rope round a stout oak tree.

The village boys too played football and cricket. The cricket team was captained by Lionel's eldest son Eddy, who always seemed determined to hit a six or be clean bowled, both of which he usually achieved in short order – a metaphor, some might say, for the way he led his life. He was, however, scrupulously fair: when in later years the bank team came down from New Court, it always somehow ended in a carefully arranged draw.

The village school educated the children under the firm eye of the schoolmaster and vicar, while the surrounding fields and the shoreline of the Beaulieu River were a huge playground for the children. Each Christmas Lionel gave every household a joint of beef and Mariloo gave every child under 14 a special present of their choice.

'Banker by hobby… gardener by profession' · Lionel at Exbury, 1919–1929

As Lionel worked in the bank during the week, the weekends – though these often included Friday afternoon and Monday morning – were his Exbury days. The head gardener was expected to be on duty. A typical message would read: 'I shall arrive at Exbury tomorrow (Friday) about 12 o'clock – will you please meet me in the glade with your staff.' With his walking stick at the ready, Lionel bluntly pointed out what should go where and, equally importantly, what needed to go on the bonfire; his was a rigorous selection programme. Often out in the gardens until sunset, he had to be called back up to the house to meet his weekend guests.

Lionel belonged to a family famous for its hospitality. The great houses of Gunnersbury, Ascott, Halton and Waddesdon Manor were the settings for frequent house parties where the family entertained their guests in style. After the war, the custom of having guests to stay for prolonged periods in the season gradually shortened to hosting weekend house parties. The brevity of a three-day stay suited Lionel well. Guests would motor down or were collected from the Beaulieu Road train station. While these weekend house parties might to some extent follow the usual schedule of country pursuits and socialising, in spring the primary focus was always the garden and here Lionel was indefatigable. In the evening there would be a welcome dinner prepared by the French chef and afterwards a film projector was set up in the drawing room for guests to watch a film sent down from London and to allow the more elderly – or weary – to snooze.

Usually the fare was pretty bland, but on one occasion, something rather more risqué (by the standards of the day) found its way down. The film – the story of Don Juan – was watched in stony silence. The next day, Mariloo recalled, P.D. Williams broke the ice by brushing away a large bumblebee from one of the rhododendron blooms, saying with characteristic humour, 'These large Don Juans with their hob-nailed boots fertilise all the wrong rhododendrons!' That night Lionel saw to it that his guests watched an innocuous Wild West film.

Some weekends were more specialised, with famed amateur garden owners, members of the Rhododendron Society (which later became the Rhododendron Association), plant hunters and officials from Kew, Edinburgh and the RHS all being welcomed to Exbury. These gardening weekends would involve intense exchanges of opinion on the latest arrivals from abroad, new propagation techniques or the treatment of diseases, along with a tour of the garden – with a little friendly competition thrown in for good measure. Lionel's generosity knew no bounds: he gave away trays of his seedlings and would sometimes name a particular rhododendron after one of his guests.

John Barr Stevenson (1882–1950), of Tower Court, Ascot, visited in spring 1921 and afterwards wrote an effusive letter of thanks: 'I do not know how to thank you sufficiently for giving me one of the happiest and most interesting weekends I have ever spent. You have no idea how I appreciated seeing the opening stages of your very great conception at Exbury ... I am sure all lovers of nature ought to be thankful that it has fallen into such excellent hands.' This was high praise indeed. Stevenson's rare collection was world-renowned: he provided many of the stock plants of the 'Wilson Fifty' Kurume azaleas, which were propagated to form the 'Punchbowl' in The Valley Garden, adjoining The Savill Gardens, Windsor after the war. After his

70

below · Mariloo giving prizes at the village fete   *opposite* · The Bog Garden, showing the giant leaves of *Gunnera manicata*

death all his species of rhododendrons – on which he was a particular expert – were painstakingly transplanted there too.

The structure and the planting of the gardens certainly developed rapidly. Writing some 30 years later, Mariloo recalled, 'In 1923 this wilderness had been transformed into a shapely garden ... and Lionel's gardening hobby had really begun to take hold of him in earnest'. More than a hobby perhaps: all his spare time was spent on developing his garden; in fact in later life he referred to himself as 'a banker by hobby but a gardener by profession'. That said, he was all too aware of how lucky he was. Furthermore, Lionel wanted to share his enthusiasm with all his guests, though not all responded equally.

In 1924 Winston Churchill (1874–1965) and his wife, Clementine (1885–1977), came to stay for a weekend; plant hunter Frank Kingdon-Ward (1885–1958) and Kew Director W.J. Bean (1863–1947) were also among the guests. Whenever he visited, Bean was always bombarded with questions but he was famously cautious in committing himself to a definitive answer. On the Sunday Churchill – no doubt suffering from 'rhododendron-itis' as Mariloo called it – slipped off to paint in the morning and retired to play cards in the afternoon while the experts marched back into the fray. He nevertheless recovered enough to captivate his audience until 3 am, as Lionel reported to Mariloo, who had long since gone to bed.

73

above · Lionel, second from left and Mariloo, second from right, showing guests the Rock Garden

right · Lionel feeding a robin

'Banker by hobby ... gardener by profession' · Lionel at Exbury, 1919–1929

Exbury attracted lovers of gardening from all walks of life –
up to and including the Royal Family. In 1925, Lionel and Mariloo
entertained Queen Mary for tea while King George V was racing
his yacht at Cowes Week. She must have enjoyed it as she came
again a few years later, in 1931, with the King, and other royals
followed, notably George VI and Queen Elizabeth (then still
Duke and Duchess of York) in 1936.

When the family were away, local horticultural societies and
members of The Gardeners' Royal Benevolent Institution were
allowed to visit the gardens privately, led by the head gardener.
The gardens were also opened in the summer months to raise
money for local charities. Mariloo was head of the local Women's
Institute and gave an annual garden party where members were
taken around the gardens. Another tea party was given for the
Royal South Hants Hospital, and on Wednesday afternoons in June
and Saturday afternoons from mid-July to August, the gardens
were open to visitors. The entrance charge was a shilling (plus
3d if coming by boat), with all proceeds going to the hospital.
Azaleas, which taxonomically fall into the rhododendron genus,
had already come into the picture and little by little Lionel also
became a connoisseur of genera other than rhododendrons,
selecting rare trees and shrubs that provided variety and a range

74

VIEWS OF OUR READERS

EXBURY HOUSE GARDENS.
To the Editor of the "Hampshire Advertiser."

Dear Sir,—In response to a request from General Byron I have decided to open the gardens at Exbury every Wednesday afternoon between the hours of three and six, from the 4th June to the 9th July, both dates inclusive.

From Tuesday, the 15th July, to Saturday, the 30th August, both dates inclusive, the gardens will be open and Saturday, between the hours of three and six.

During the month of September the gardens will only be open on the first and third Wednesdays.

A fee of 1s. per person will be charged for admission, the whole of this money going to the Southampton Hospital Re-Building Fund.

Launches conveying visitors to the grounds will be allowed to unload at my private pier at an extra charge of 3d. per person.

Yours truly,
LIONEL DE ROTHSCHILD.
Exbury House,
Exbury,
Southampton.
27th, May, 1930.

above · Lionel opened the gardens for charity as well as welcoming private guests

of colour. The garden expanded into Witcher's Wood, named after a local family of charcoal burners, a common trade in the New Forest. Witcher's Wood lies between Daffodil Meadow, with its view of the Beaulieu River, and the main drive. Lover's Lane runs down it to the jetty Lionel built. To the left of it lies Lady Chamberlain Walk, named after Lady Ivy Chamberlain (1878–1941), the sister-in-law of Neville Chamberlain (1869–1940), down which Lionel planted his exquisite bell-shaped *R. cinnabarinum* hybrids, R.'Lady Berry', R.'Lady Rosebery' and the eponymous R.'Lady Chamberlain' itself. All three have won FCCs but sadly they and their parent, *R. cinnabarinum*, can be susceptible to powdery mildew. Several of Lionel's favourite magnolias also grow today in Witcher's Wood, including *Magnolia macrophylla*, a deciduous magnolia from America with the largest single leaves and simple flowers of any tree or shrub hardy in the British Isles. Lionel planted three *Magnolia macrophylla* but they were, as he put it, 'not an easy subject' to grow from seed.

Occasionally Lionel would buy whole plant collections, perhaps because the owner was under financial pressure, or was finding it hard to cope with old age or had simply died. In 1926 the Lowinsky rhododendrons from Tittenhurst Park in Sunninghill were acquired this way by Lionel and J.J. Crosfield of Embley Park, Hampshire, who chose the best plants for their gardens. The stud book has been mislaid, but it is known that Lionel was delighted with some 'outstanding and very beautiful seedlings' and these were mainly planted in Witcher's Wood.

Slowly and carefully Lionel was transforming more woodland to showcase his beloved rhododendrons, azaleas and many other acid-loving plants. He ensured that many other complementary plants were grown in Exbury and he had a distinct sense of place, variety and colour in ordering his planting to give interest from spring through to autumn. He also took special care in the structure of his planting. The upper high canopy of the established trees gave protection from the wind and shade from the sun. Under this a middle layer of smaller trees and larger leaved rhododendrons sheltered and a lower tier of smaller trees and shrubs such as camellias, magnolias, cherries, cotoneaster, viburnum and berberis gave texture and colour. Finally all was underplanted with bulbs and herbaceous woodland plants that enjoyed the moist ground beneath.

QUAY & PIER AT GILBURY.

above and right · R.'Lady Chamberlain'; Gilbury Pier at the end of Lover's Lane

Rock gardens had been a feature of gardening since the eighteenth century and the fashion for them reached a pinnacle in the inter-war period, spurred on by the introductions of Reginald Farrer (1880–1920). Elsewhere in Rothschild gardens, notably at Waddesdon in the late nineteenth century, Pulhamite stone had been used to great effect; this was a mix of brick and clinker covered with a Portland cement mixture and modelled into sandstone or limestone-effect boulders. There had also been a rock grotto and cascades at Gunnersbury Park. Exbury, however, led the way in its large-scale naturalistic interpretation of the conditions of the Himalayas rather than opting for the more whimsical features – such as a scale model of the Matterhorn – which appeared in gardens around England. In fact, the eminent RHS historian Dr Brent Elliott has described the Exbury Rock Garden as '[a]mong the most notable rock gardens of the interwar years' and 'probably the largest rock garden of its kind in Europe'.

A 'mass attack of the Chelsea rock gardens' resulted in many of the leading alpine nurseries, including James Backhouse and Son, Symons-Jeune and Clarence Elliott Ltd, becoming popular staples of the RHS Great Spring Shows. Elliott (awarded the RHS Victoria Medal of Honour in 1951) was a plant hunter who collected with Farrer in the Alps and a founder member of the Alpine Garden Society. He was one of the most consistent show contributors and, meeting at the RHS Hall, Lionel struck up a conversation with Elliott at his alpine exhibit. Lionel said, with an air of regret, '[I]t's no use my looking at your alpines – I have no rock garden,' and then added, 'but if ever I make one you shall build it.'

He was as good as his word. Lionel had distinct ideas of what type of rock garden he wished to create. The purpose of the rock garden was to be a setting for his Himalayan rhododendrons, such as *R. sanguineum*, *R. lapponicum* and *R. saluenense*, which did not like the shaded woods and would prefer a more light and open site. Elliott was invited down for an Exbury weekend and soon after he was commissioned to design the project. Lionel and Elliott agreed that the two-and-a-half-acre site of a disused gravel pit would be used to create the rocky outcrops with a 'kind of ravine' to emulate the alpine conditions.

In 1929 the project started but Elliott was due to leave for a plant-hunting expedition in Chile to collect for Lionel, so he left the rock garden in the capable hands of his foreman E.K. Balls (1892–1984): 'the best Rock builder I know ... he will be very ready to get your specialised views in connection with the work and to work to them'. Elliott and Balls may have been brought in from outside, but Lionel's existing team of Exbury labourers, who were already on site, did all the groundwork. On visiting in March 1930 Elliott was impressed by the progress of the garden, saying: 'You must have given Mr Balls a very good gang of men.'

below · The construction of the Rock Garden   *opposite* · *R. luteiflorum*   *previous and following pages* · *see page 197*

Limestone was a fashionable material at the time, but Elliott recommended 'a fine rough sandstone, weathering well and entirely suitable', which he sourced from Wales. Suitable it may have been but there was a lot of it. That October, the vast quantities of stone started to arrive at Exbury by road in 100-ton loads. A specially constructed light railway was used to move them from the estate yard where they were offloaded to the disused gravel pit; many of the rocks could weigh up to five or six tons apiece. Given the size of the site and the weight of the rocks, each one of which had to be carefully lowered into position: a steel crane with a 60-foot jib was bought specially for the project. Lionel eventually wrote, a little anxiously, to Elliott on 19 August 1929, 'I take it that when you have reached the first 1,000 tons you will cry a halt for me to decide how much further I am going.' His anxiety was well founded: it took double that to complete – and four years before the project was finished and all traces of its extraordinary construction removed. Years later, Elliott remembered Lionel fondly: 'he was the most satisfactory and generous man I ever worked for. He wanted the best, knew when he had got the best, and paid on the level best without

question. He was that extremely rare thing, a very wealthy man who realised that for work carried out one was entitled to a decent profit, and he sincerely wished and expected one to make it.' Elliott also added, 'Exbury week-ends were delightful, intensely interesting and utterly exhausting.'

A water supply was buried under the rock and spray apparatus procured from the British Overhead Irrigation Company to keep the plants dampened on a weekly basis. The surrounding oak trees and newly-planted *Pinus radiata* gave shelter from the wind. Lionel also planted a fringe of R. *yunnanese* to give a band of lighter foliage and flowers against the darker R. *discolor* hybrids that surrounded the area. He was very clear, however, that this was not to be 'an Alpine rock-garden': he wanted a setting for dwarf species of rhododendrons.

Lionel used plants he had grown at Exbury from the seeds collected by his plant hunters (whose invaluable contribution we discuss in Chapter 6). In placing them, again he was a perfectionist: he moved plants around to their optimum positions, finding the colour and growth combinations a continual balancing act as they acclimatised to their English setting. Some plants were planted initially at the bottom

of the rock garden, but were moved to higher ground, whereas others enjoyed the slightly boggy soil. The R. *fragariiflorum* which Kingdon-Ward collected in South East Tibet in 1924, with 'crushed strawberry colour flowers', proved to be 'the least happy'. Lionel reported, 'I do not think I have yet got the right place for it'. As for the R. *leucaspis* which Kingdon-Ward took a liking to for its foliage alone, without having seen it flower, Lionel marvelled that it 'seems as happy in our climate as in the Tsangpo Gorges'.

Despite descriptions from the plant hunters of the plants in their native habitat, the anticipated colours of the seedlings could be diverse. The rock garden became a show of pinks, purples, and

yellows and Lionel's work epitomised Kingdon-Ward's view of rock gardens, when he said, 'Here is no crude imitation of nature but rather a most fastidious selection and recombination of line, form, colour, like a Chinese painting, to produce a completely satisfying harmony.'

Honey fungus took its toll – as did the openness of the site, occasional waterlogging and frost. 'Gardening would be too easy if it was always a success', Lionel noted wryly. However, his project was feted in the gardening press, and Lionel could proudly bring his gardening guests to see yet another extraordinary feature he had successfully created at Exbury.

The garden comes of age

EXBURY IN THE 1930S

CHAPTER 5

By the end of the 1920s Lionel's plant collections were expanding at such a rapid pace that he needed more room. Adjoining the Rock Garden lay Yard Wood, so called – supposedly – after the 'yardsticks' used in archery; the wood was full of yews, a wood often used to make longbows.

One problem was the public road, Gilbury Lane, which ran down to some land and houses Lionel did not own and separated Yard Wood from the rest of the garden. After several years of opening and closing gates in order to cross it, he built a balustraded bridge, high across the lane, from limestone ashlar. Gilbury Bridge is a fine feature: two truly magnificent fastigiate beeches, *Fagus sylvatica* 'Dawyck', flank the approach on the house side, while huge examples of *Magnolia* x *veitchii* 'Peter Veitch' show their pink flowers against the pale blue sky of early spring, followed in mid-season by various cultivars of the R. Naomi Group, a lovely pink rhododendron named after Lionel's younger daughter, and smaller *R. williamsianum* hybrids, with their characteristic rounded leaves.

Yard Wood today contains the autumn colours of Exbury's National Collection of *Nyssa* and *Oxydendrum*. Lionel too collected plants for their autumn colour, admiring the lovely *Liquidambar* and *Quercus coccinea* among others. Some years after work first started in Yard Wood, and with his now experienced eye, Lionel would create the peaceful scene that was Jubilee Pond, named in commemoration of the Silver Jubilee of George V in 1935, with rivulets trickling down the sloping landscape of flowering cherries and maples.

82

this page
R. 'Naomi Paris'; Gilbury bridge under construction, and complete

opposite
M. x *veitchii* 'Peter Veitch'

Chapter Five

From the eighteenth century many large landowners had taken to the fashion of creating a pinetum or arboretum to display recently acquired North American exotic trees to their best effect. This trend was encouraged in the nineteenth century by the plant nurseries such as Veitch, Loddiges and Hilliers. Early contemporaries of Lionel, such as the Holfords at Westonbirt, the Loders at Wakehurst Place and the Messels at Nymans, all developed their arboretums in this period. Lionel chose land to the north-east of the house in 1929 to embark on his own. He was nothing if not ambitious: he wanted to plant every hardy tree and shrub listed in W.J. Bean's seminal book, *Trees and Shrubs Hardy in the British Isles*, first published in 1914 and updated at intervals thereafter; Bean himself was to advise.

This was no small undertaking. Dynamite was used to blow holes in the rough agricultural ground in order to give the root balls of the huge number of trees a good start. The more exposed conditions of the fields were tricky; many larger specimens such as *Aesculus turbinata*, *Pinus radiata* and *Cupressus macrocarpa* would, as Lionel put it, 'if planted in trenched ground grow too quickly and tumble over from their own weight or are blown over in the slightest sign of a gale'. An aerial photograph of the arboretum taken by the Luftwaffe on reconnaissance in 1943 shows just how large a scheme it was, well over 100 acres with long *allées* in an arched grid crossed with paths radiating around a central point. The whole enterprise survived the war and a photograph from 1953 shows trees unkempt but starting to mature, but then – tragically – it was grubbed up for farmland.

At the bottom of Home Wood, Lionel found that the micro-climate offered warmer air than elsewhere in the gardens, ideal for the early-flowering and large-leaved rhododendrons. He called this area the Winter Garden; he had already planted some special trees around there. These included one of the rarest and loveliest trees in the garden, the pink-flowered *Magnolia insignis* (formerly *Manglietia insignis*), grown from seed he received from

opposite · Gilbury bridge and the fastigiate beeches in autumn below · Aerial photograph of Lionel's arboretum, 1953

The garden comes of age · Exbury in the 1930s

the plant hunter Reginald Farrer in 1919, which he surrounded with the sweet-smelling R. *crassum* at its base, and the carmine cherry, *Prunus cerasoides*, which its collector Kingdon-Ward described as 'the most splendid tree I ever saw in the wild'.

Here too he planted scented witch hazels – still there – and of course early flowering rhododendrons that he wanted to be protected from the frost, like the pretty R. *moupinense*, later adding his own hybrids, like R. 'Bric-à-brac'. In due course this became the main location for his large-leaved rhododendrons. The canopy of oaks and other indigenous trees provided them with shade and offered wind protection, so in time they gained the treelike stature found in their native habitat of the Himalayas, though in some cases they can take a good many years before they first flower. The enormous R. 'Fortune', created at Exbury using R. *sinogrande* pollen collected from the garden of George Johnstone (1882–1960) at Trewithen, Cornwall, is one of the highlights. Mariloo recorded the first appearance of the splendid primrose-yellow bloom in 1938. 'As we walked into the woods we saw this magnificent plant holding up its glorious blooms to a deep-blue sky. In the evening Lionel gathered his family to a round-table conference to discuss the merits of the new seedling, looking most majestic. Not only was the flower outstanding, but its great leaves were disposed so as to remind me of the Discobolus, the Greek thrower of the discus with arm stretched out and poised for the throw.'

The original Heather Garden at Exbury was a fashionable, early spring feature, which had a long history in past gardening styles. Hardy heaths have been in cultivation since Philip Miller's curatorship of the Chelsea Physic Garden in the eighteenth century and a formal Heath Garden was recorded at the Duke of Bedford's seat, Woburn Abbey, in 1825. The term 'Heath' relates to the Erica genus and 'Heather' to the Calluna genus: though botanically different, they have many characteristics in common; the latter are generally twice the size of the former. The Victorians treated heathers as temporary bedding plants to fill in areas when the more exotic specimens were over, but by the Edwardian period, the Heath Garden, like the Bamboo Garden or the Water Garden (all found at Gunnersbury), was a popular feature.

Lionel himself propagated and grew his heathers in his cool glasshouses. At the Empire Exhibition at Wembley in 1924–1925, he saw the South African government's display of indigenous plants, including nerines and ericas; later, in 1936, he obtained hardy ericas such as *Erica pageana*, E. *fervida* and E. *pillansii* from the Stellenbosch, in exchange for amaryllis bulbs.

Not surprisingly, R. 'Fortune' won an FCC when shown that year. Lionel planted groups of these statuesque rhododendrons and their 40 foot height, gigantic leaves and beautiful blooms have been an attraction ever since.

The garden comes of age · Exbury in the 1930s

above · Lionel's photograph of Villa Carlotta on Lake Como   *opposite* · The Italian garden to the east of Exbury House; R.'Yellow Hammer', a lepidote hybrid

Lionel's love of the Italian lakes and their more formal gardens may have inspired the creation of the Italian Garden that sits beside the house. Using the south-facing wall along the staff wing of Exbury house, it was possible to create a warm, intimate space with two formal, contemplative pools where waterlilies – much prized by his father at Gunnersbury – were planted with spring tulips, climbers across the walls, and carnations as summer cuttings in the borders.

Lionel knew the iris expert William Dykes (1877–1925), a friend of his cousin Charles Rothschild (1877–1923), himself a knowledgeable entomologist and iris-lover at Ashton Wold, Northamptonshire. Charles had a formidable collection and

after his early death in 1923, it was bequeathed to Kew (he had already given many from his travels in Europe). Lionel too loved irises, ordering many from his suppliers for planting in the Iris Garden; this was a natural feature with a boggy soil and shady location, and thus a perfect place to plant iris species and hybrids. The Iris Garden fell into some disrepair after the war but was restored and enlarged in time for the Centenary.

In addition to his keen landscaping eye and his urge to collect examples of everything possible, for Lionel the 'great excitement' (as he put it) was breeding new plants. 'Gardeners are not usually gamblers', he wrote, 'but yet there are very few human beings who do not get some pleasure out of a little gamble some time in their lives.' For him, this gamble was the raising of species and hybrids from seed, above all the latter. His mentor, J.C. Williams, was perhaps a little more sanguine, writing, 'Start hybridising rhododendrons. It's the greatest fun. You get ten, fifteen, perhaps twenty years of pleasurable anticipation, and only *one* day of disappointment – the day your seedlings open their first flowers!' That said, J.C. also warned, 'Lionel, please give great thought to the crosses you are about to make. There are far too many rhododendron hybrids made indiscriminately.'

The early hybridists were experimenting with whatever material they could get hold of and mainly used *R. arboreum*, the blood-red species reaching 50–60 feet at its full height and growing best in the milder part of the UK; for hardiness they used *R. catawbiense* from North America and *R. caucasicum* and *R. ponticum* from the Near East. Then came the great introductions in the middle of the nineteenth century, first from Joseph Hooker's (1817–1911) expedition to the Sikkim-Himalaya in 1849 and then from Robert Fortune's (1812–1880) to China six years later.

From the early twentieth century, and the next phase of plant hunting, the Chinese, Tibetan and South-East Asian species gave a wealth of material to choose from – which is why the rhododendron was one of the most popular requests for plant hunters to collect at this time. The 312 new species introduced in the second decade of the twentieth century exceeded the entire number described up to 1900. Keen hybridists like Lionel wanted to 'put colour into the tough ones and toughness in the delicate ones'.

Taxonomy, then and now, had a bearing on what hybridists could and could not do. The genus is divided between lepidotes and elepidotes: the former, generally smaller plants, have tiny scales under the leaves; the latter are smooth. It is impossible to cross lepidote with elepidote. Much experimentation ensued with these new introductions – initially species with species or with older hybrids and then, of course, new hybrid with new hybrid as they matured. Lionel was organised and crystal clear with his hybridising. As he put it, 'Nothing was ever done haphazardly or in a makeshift manner.' The aims of the amateur rhododendron grower were slightly different from those of the commercial grower: the flower was of immediate concern. Certainly the new colour should be an improvement on the parents but, above all, it should be pure; Lionel and his friends especially eschewed the magenta found in so many Victorian hybrids. The genus is vast, ranging from large to small and from white, through pink, red,

purple, yellow – with some of the best yellows being introduced around this time – and orange. The leaves too vary, in shape and size and shade of green; some also have beautiful soft brown indumentum beneath. Occasionally Lionel grew one only for its leaves, picking off the flowers when they bloomed. As ever, he was ahead of his time: the value of their leaves has made something of a comeback in recent years, for example R. 'Bloombux', an alternative to boxwood, and Glendoick's R. 'Ever Red', which has dark leaves with a deep red underside.

Another important aim was to prolong the flowering time as much as possible, so that from Christmas until early July there would be something going on in Exbury. The hardiness that Lionel sought for his hybrids was one of the most heartfelt wishes of any rhododendron grower. For a plant to withstand climates such as the highlands of Scotland, the drought of Exbury or the rainfall of the West Midlands – and not droop or flop if rained on – was an outstanding achievement. To achieve all three was, potentially, a miracle.

Lionel and his contemporaries approached the whole business rather like his father had approached racehorses: they believed in using the best form of the plant to get the best result. He once drove to the Sunningdale Nurseries of the legendary nurseryman Harry White (1857–1938) to get some pollen from White's better form of R. dichroanthum to put on R. haematodes, producing R. 'Burning Bush'. In the case of the R. cinnabarinum hybrids mentioned earlier – R. 'Lady Chamberlain', R. 'Lady Rosebery' and R. 'Lady Berry' – he used J.C. Williams's R. 'Royal Flush'. His use of George Johnstone's R. sinogrande to produce R. 'Fortune' has already been mentioned; the same care is evident in one of his other great successes with the colour yellow, R. 'Crest'.

W.J. Bean said of Lionel, 'He was one of the first to see the potentialities of R. wardii as a parent'; in this case he made the same cross twice, a year apart. The first time his stud book specifies that he used a really good form of R. wardii collected by Kingdon-Ward (KW 4170) but the second time it is unspecified. While it is not certain, it seems likely that it was the KW 4170 R. wardii, which won an AM in 1931 and which Lionel praised so highly, that was the parent of R. 'Crest'. R. 'Hawk', which he lived to see, is a good yellow but it is far surpassed by R. 'Crest', which only flowered in the early 1950s, winning an FCC in 1953, and is still one of the best clear yellows in existence.

These are but a handful of his crosses. He let every seedling, however small or late, grow on to flowering stage but thereafter he exercised a fine discrimination: Exbury's bonfires were legendary and he wanted to ensure his garden held only the best of his work. Lionel never named a plant after himself nor allowed anyone else to do so, but he did use many family names for his hybrids, most notably R. 'Mariloo', a R. lacteum cross named after his wife, and R. 'Naomi' after his younger daughter.

opposite · R. 'Crest' above · Naomi

Competition between amateur gardeners was fierce and there was groundbreaking work going on elsewhere. The gardens at Bodnant, already very beautiful, were developed yet further by Henry McLaren, 2nd Lord Aberconway (1879–1953), 'one of the most gifted plantsmen of his generation', who embarked on his own hybridising programme in friendly rivalry with Exbury. At a rough count, Exbury accounted for some 25% of registered interwar crosses and Bodnant for a further 10% in the Stud Book of the Rhododendron Association, as published in their Year Book from 1934, though these numbers should be treated as giving only a partial picture: in keeping with their somewhat purist approach – or perhaps simply for ease of tabulation and lack of space – they only listed all primary crosses (i.e. between two species), any cross of which one parent was a species and all hybrids that had received AM or FCC awards since 1923. Even so, Lionel's programme was prolific indeed.

KNAP HILL *The deciduous azaleas*

Lionel's hybridising skills extended to azaleas too. Taxonomically, azaleas belong to the genus Rhododendron, with evergreen azaleas in the section Tsutsusi and deciduous azaleas in the section Pentanthera. For the gardener, however, the difference between an azalea and a rhododendron is easy to know but harder to describe. While Lionel undertook a little hybridisation of evergreen azaleas, it is the deciduous ones that interested him most and upon which his fame in this area rests.

Lionel saw the earlier success of the trade nurseries that had already undertaken extensive hybridisation and recognised the potential to improve them. With this in mind he turned to Waterer, a frequent supplier of the Rothschild family. The elder Lionel of Gunnersbury was a customer, as was Ferdinand, who bought plants in the late 1800s for Waddesdon Manor.

In the nineteenth century propagation was often carried out in utmost secrecy in nursery trial beds tucked away from public gaze. Anthony Waterer (c.1850–1924) at Knap Hill built upon the work of the Dutch and Belgian hybridisers but improved all the key characteristics – size, hardiness, scent, autumn foliage and, above all, flower colour. However, he did not sell them commercially.

Anthony Waterer was 'an eccentric individual' and Lionel remarked that 'he liked to gloat over the best of his azaleas and glory in their being in his collection only'. The 'favoured few' were allowed to see them but 'when one suggested that a plant would be admirable at Exbury', he would say that he had it marked out for his own garden, where he grew a few herbaceous plants and vegetables, 'but *never* an azalea'.

By the 1900s, however, these azaleas had finally started to circulate and P.D. Williams expressed his delight at their array of colours, 'crimson deep and solid, the scarlets brilliant as a new hunting coat, the yellows attaining the colour of rich Guernsey butter, the oranges bright with crimson filaments to the anthers and of course there were beautiful pinks and whites'.

Lionel acquired a batch in 1920 and some more arrived at Exbury after Anthony's death in 1924. Anthony's brother Hosea Waterer (1852–1926) returned from America to run the nursery but died soon after and his sons put the nursery up for sale. Lionel seized the opportunity and purchased the nursery in 1930.

Exbury soon received a batch of Knap Hill azaleas including R.'George Reynolds' which was an 'outstanding soft yellow and pink with a wavy petalled flower that sometimes measured six inches across'. Lionel crossed this with some of Waterer's unnamed orange deep-blotched seedlings. R.'Hotspur' was the result, winning an RHS Award of Merit in 1934. Yet again, Lionel found that 'the better the parent, the better its offspring'. He also found that 'the simile of the paint box' did not hold, and it was better to cross 'like with like'.

In his Exbury azalea crosses, he created brilliant colours: they range from the hot orange and apricot through salmon, rose and silvery pink to white.

below, from left · R. 'Hotspur Orange'; R. 'Basilisk'; R. 'Cecile'   above · Deciduous azaleas at the Top Pond

Lionel did not stop there. He continued to invest in the nursery as he sought to combine his hybridisation work at Exbury with the commercial scale of Knap Hill. He charged 10% commission on his plants sold through the nursery but, indul-gently perhaps, bought plants back from Knap Hill for Exbury.

In 1931, to further assist Knap Hill's development, a fresh business partnership between Robert Jenkinson (1900–1970) and a member of another branch of the Waterer family, Frank Gomer Waterer (1867–1945), was initiated by Lionel. Gomer, as he was usually known, was the grandson of John Waterer of the competing Bagshot nursery (then called John Waterer, Sons & Crisp), an experienced grower and excellent salesman, who had travelled extensively to America. He had inherited his ancestor's talent and had raised some notable rhododendrons, most notably of all, R. 'Pink Pearl', which won an FCC in 1900 and became one of the most popular nursery hybrids of the day.

Jenkinson was a charming plantsman who enjoyed creating nursery catalogues with tempting bulletins on the latest plants and he added new commercially viable strains to the Knap Hill hybridising programme. It was also Jenkinson's idea to appoint a nursery manager, Frank Knight (1903–1985), who had trained at Werrington and worked at Kew and who would eventually go on to become Director of the RHS garden at Wisley. In 1935 a devastating frost at Knap Hill destroyed the flowers of every azalea on open ground: with characteristic generosity, Lionel immediately invited them down to make crosses at Exbury using azaleas he had acquired from Anthony Waterer all those years before.

However, the nursery struggled to become financially viable despite all their talents and a substantial investment to support Knap Hill was needed from Lionel in 1936. Lionel did not live to see the nursery back into profit and Gomer died just before peace was declared. G. Donald Waterer (1913–2006) returned from prisoner-of-war camp and began the task of restoring it to its former glory. Lionel's sons continued to invest in a small way until well into the 1960s but then the link ceased and the firm went its own way.

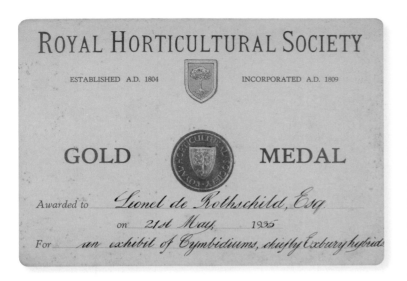

Lionel regularly exhibited at the RHS Flower shows to inspire others – and celebrate his own achievements – winning many prizes and awards for his rhododendrons and orchids, whether in display or for individual plants. Preparations for the Chelsea Flower Shows started months in advance and the Exbury exhibits were always in the large marquee beside the main drive. Competition for awards between the amateur growers of rhododendrons was increasingly fierce. The year 1937 was exceptional as it was Coronation year: there was a celebratory atmosphere in the marquees and fine weather graced the opening private view day. Lionel was duly honoured with the Cain Cup, this time for his colourful exhibit of azalea hybrids – in 1930 he had won it for orchids – with his friend Lord Aberconway coming in second place.

Two of the most prestigious RHS show cups were donated by Lionel and are still awarded: the Rothschild Challenge Cup is given to the best exhibit where rhododendrons predominate, and the Lionel de Rothschild Cup is presented for the best exhibit of six species. Lionel always gave a dinner for all involved in the exhibition, from competitors to those working behind the scenes.

Competing at the RHS Flower shows took a lot of hard work – some years more than others. One year, when a frost damaged the exhibit the day before opening, the response was an impressive one. A quick phone call and fifteen lorries left Exbury with dug-up shrubs at 4 o'clock in the morning to mount a 'staggering' display. Lionel was very much at the centre of it all, but he was well served by his head gardeners, first by Kneller and then by Bedford. Sadly, on returning from London in 1934, Arthur Bedford sat down on a bench and died of a heart attack: his last words were variously recorded as 'Another Chelsea Flower Show over' or 'This field is full of daisies'. He was sorely missed.

Lionel also applied his skills to the growing of camellias. When they first arrived in England in the 1730s, camellias were thought too tender and considered suitable only for the greenhouse, but this was soon proved wrong and their cultivation flourished, especially in Cornwall. Lionel admired them as an early herald of spring, and they liked the mild climate of Exbury. The original Camellia Walk, in the eastern side of Home Wood, was planted in the 1930s and included a number of his Exbury hybrids. Camellias at Exbury have been much expanded since, first with the New Camellia Walk that runs parallel to it and more recently with the Gilbury Lane Garden. There are now over 740 different camellia varieties thriving in the shady woodland conditions throughout the garden.

Lionel also planted many magnolias to be enjoyed by future generations, including the early flowering *Magnolia campbellii* in the Home Wood, a beautiful sight in early spring against a clear blue sky. He planted the Japanese summer-flowering *M. obovata*, with its huge leaves and scented flowers and the hardier, early-blooming *M.* x *soulangeana*, while at Gilbury Bridge he planted *M.* x *veitchii* 'Peter Veitch', towering spectacularly above the rhododendrons and azaleas. Many more have now been added, especially in New Camellia Walk, and Lionel would have delighted in the different colours – white, pink, deep purple and yellow. The flash of pure yellow seems a particular goal for the woodland gardener: for Lionel it was the search for a good yellow rhododendron hybrid, as we have seen. Since the 1990s there have been ever more brilliant yellow magnolias. Now, with new species from China and Vietnam, the race is on to produce hardy yellow camellias. Lionel would have loved it.

Cotoneasters were a favourite genus of Lionel due to their attractive berries. They were also another genus with which to experiment. To his contacts at Kew and Edinburgh he said, 'I am very interested in Cotoneasters at the present time and am trying to get a representative collection. I notice there are a good many in your list that I have not got and, as you know, the obscure varieties cannot be purchased.' By the 1930s, W.J. Bean reported in the *New Flora and Silva* that he had seen *C. glabratus* 'at Exbury [where] it grows luxuriantly 10 feet or more high and bears very plentiful crops of berries. Mr de Rothschild regards it as one of his very best of his extensive collection of Chinese cotoneasters.'

Lionel's successful Exbury hybrids included the yellow fruiting, wildlife-friendly *C.* 'Exburiensis' – 'a sight not easily forgotten and a pleasant change from the scarlets and crimsons' – and *C.* 'Rothschildianus', again with yellow fruits. Not that he ignored red: he also produced the beautiful and popular *C.* 'Cornubia', which won an FCC in 1936. Both *C.* 'Rothschildianus' and *C.* 'Cornubia' hold the coveted Award of Garden Merit (AGM), ensuring their continued popularity and availability. Not all his plants have stood the test of time, however: a berberis (or 'barberry' as he called it) that he presented at the Tree and Shrub Conference of 1938, honouring it with the name B. 'Exburiensis', appears to be lost to cultivation.

To a list that includes rhododendrons, camellias, azaleas and magnolias we can also add orchids. In fact, the Rothschild name has long been associated with orchids, and two of the most famous – still – are the rare long-whiskered *Paphiopedilum*

rothschildianum and the popular purple *Vanda* Rothschildiana. In the Exbury glasshouses Lionel maintained the family passion for orchids.

In 1928 Lionel was invited onto the RHS Orchid Committee by the chairman, Jeremiah Colman (1859–1942). Colman, of Gatton Park in Surrey, had an extensive orchid collection with over 30,000 species and 25,000 hybrids. Lionel was a natural choice due to his family's long association with the genus and his achievements with his rhododendron hybrids. Lionel soon assumed the position of Vice-Chairman of the Orchid Committee. He had brought some orchids with him from Gunnersbury but now he set about establishing his collection with multiple and large purchases at auction, and from orchid suppliers, of the very best cymbidiums, cattleyas, odontoglossums, cypripediums, miltonias and calanthes.

Chapter Five

There were many unanswered questions about the anatomy and propagation of the genus that fascinated orchid enthusiasts. Lionel wanted to create his own hybrids and multiply them through the so far unproven process of propagation by seed. He was used to a waiting game with his rhododendrons and to achieve this – and claim the scientific and commercial breakthrough – was tempting indeed.

Orchid seed germination had been successfully tested in 1890 by Lionel's cousin Edmond de Rothschild (1845–1934) at Armainvilliers near Paris, where he had raised the first known artificial odontoglossum hybrid, *Odontoglossum* Leroyanum. He followed the wisdom of Noel Bernard (1874–1911), a French scientist who had discovered the phenomenon of the symbiotic germination of orchids. Edmond had a laboratory at Armainvilliers, where a secret formula of carrot juice, sugar and *agar agar* (seaweed) led his head gardener to claim that these were the first aseptic trials of their kind with orchid seeds.

Other methods considered by Lionel were the Burgeff formula, based on the findings of Hans Burgeff (1883–1976),

a German botanist who experimented with orchid seeds and mycorrhizal fungi, and the American Lewis Knudson's (1884–1958) successful non-fungi formula. In England, notable members of the RHS Orchid Committee, Bruno Schroder (1867–1940) and Frederick Hanbury (1851–1935), were trialling orchid seed germination in their private laboratories. Trade suppliers were experimenting in symbiotic germination too. However, the reality was that no one was near to finding an infallible process.

Lionel was able to use a spare laboratory at the Royal Mint Refinery (RMR) for his first orchid experiments. The Refinery's chemical processes and testing were perfectly aligned with the sterile environment needed for orchid seed germination. The Rothschilds had operated the bullion refinery near Tower Bridge since 1852 and it was a thriving business. After the death of Charles Rothschild in 1923, Lionel and his younger brother Anthony had taken control and improvements were carried out – including new laboratory space.

Although no photographs remain, the carefully written laboratory germination

procedures allow one to imagine the professional set-up of Lionel's orchid laboratory. Williams, his 'good chemicals man', was given the task of carrying out the trials with the different formulas. Orders for chemicals were placed through the Refinery account books and seeds were obtained from trade suppliers in exchange for the subsequent seedlings. The results were recorded in an 'LR'-filled stud book. Once at seedling stage, the plants were carefully taken down to the Exbury orchid glasshouses that were soon burgeoning with new orchid hybrids flowering on a grand scale.

Benjamin Hills (1884–1960) had worked for 17 years under

H.G. Alexander (1875–1972), the orchid grower for Sir George Holford (1860–1926) and the man who was responsible for one of the most famous cymbidiums of all time, *Cymbidium* Alexanderi 'Westonbirt'. Lionel was delighted to have obtained Hills' services, enabling him to fast-track orchid cultivation at Exbury. Hills would give 22 years of service to Exbury and grew hybrids 'in the old-fashioned way', while his daughter Evelyn (1915–2009) raised thousands of plants in the orchid laboratory.

opposite · Lachenalias and Cotoneasters, *see page 196*

99

The orchid experiments continued at the RMR until 1933 when the whole operation was moved down to Exbury. Williams visited the laboratory in July of that year and recorded that the newly installed electric heating equipment at Exbury was far better than the Refinery's gas.

Exbury's award-winning collection included those of other people, like Cymbidium Apollo and the renowned tetraploid, *Cym*. Rosanna 'Pinkie' from H.G. Alexander or *Cym*. Swallow from Sanders of St Albans (the extraordinary family firm of Sanders were to orchids as Waterers were to rhododendrons). These and

Lionel's own lovely hybrids, like *Cymbidium* Balkis (using *Cym*. Rosanna 'Pinkie') and *Cym*. Nan Kham, were hailed as 'example[s] of his exceptional skill from which every cymbidium enthusiast has benefited'.

The emerging importance of science cannot be overstated. Many cymbidiums at the time were diploids, having two chromosomes, characterised as having a more free-growing habit, more flowers per spike and more variety of colour types. Tetraploids, having four chromosomes, were rarer: in addition to *Cym*. Rosanna 'Pinkie', *Cym*. Alexanderi 'Westonbirt' was also one.

They tended to have fewer but larger flowers and, of course, having twice the chromosomes of their diploid counterparts could exert twice the genetic influence.

Most modern cymbidiums are the result of mating tetraploid with diploid, thus getting the advantages of both, albeit that the resulting triploids are themselves usually sterile. As with his rhododendrons, Lionel delighted in showing his orchids, mounting spectacular displays and winning many cups and medals from the RHS, as well as numerous AMs and FCCs for individual plants.

The orchid collection was extraordinary but Exbury also excelled in the growing of other glasshouse plants. The collection of hippeastrums, for instance, resided in a glasshouse of its own; they were referred to by Lionel, in common with others at the time, as 'amaryllis'. Botanically that term is now reserved for outdoor plants of South African origin and 'hippeastrum' for indoor plants of South American origin, like these. It was 'believed to be the very best in the country', due to Lionel's ingenuity in obtaining the brilliant Westonbirt collection (possibly through Hills), so all of his best hybrids had Holford bulbs as a parent. Lionel crossed them with those of his uncle Alfred from Halton. To show them at their most floriferous he would retard the plants so they would flower for the Chelsea Flower Show in May, choosing from the 1,100 flowering bulbs of his own making; a particularly lovely one named after his daughter Rosemary was shown in 1931. He also made a handful of crosses with clivias and daffodils and considerably more with the lovely South African bulb, *Nerine sarniensis*.

These nerine hybrids came into their own after the war and, as we shall see, it is on them that Exbury's glasshouse fame now chiefly rests. However, in Lionel's day it was orchids: the glasshouse collections would eventually total some 28,000 orchids in 1940, of which 19,000 were cymbidums and the rest comprised odontoglossums, miltonias, cattleyas, vandas, phalaenopses, paphiopedilums (then called cypripediums) and odontiodas.

The arrival of the Second World War spelt the end of orchid-growing. Economies were made, fuel rationed, glasshouse staff went to war and growing vegetables soon became a priority over growing flowers. Lionel was keen to find an American buyer for the whole lot or even the larger part, but the price offered was not good and perhaps he was unconvinced that a new owner would look after his orchids in the way he had. He therefore reluctantly made the decision to break up the collection. Many were given to Kew and many more auctioned by Protheroe and Morris in April 1940, with proceeds going to the Red Cross. Approximately six hundred were sent to the Queen. Enough remained – paphiopedilums, cattleyas and above all cymbidiums – to mount good exhibits at the shows even in the 1950s, but the collection was gradually sold and wound down, coming to an end in the 1960s.

The feats of scientific enquiry, hybridising, breeding, planting, sharing knowledge and sheer hard work that produced so many extraordinary and award-winning plants at Exbury are impressive in themselves. However, this could not have happened without the plant hunters, who played such a major role in many of Exbury's achievements and who take centre stage in the next chapter.

101

Pioneers
and plant hunters

EXPEDITIONS, NEAR AND FAR

CHAPTER 6

Chapter Six

R. Chartophyllum. Franch var praecox. Diels.

left and opposite
Photographs taken by
George Forrest on his
1918–19 expedition

previous pages · see page 197

'The plant collector's job is to uncover the hidden
beauties of the world, so that others may share his joy.'
Frank Kingdon-Ward

Plant hunting is centuries old, pioneered by missionaries, priests and botanists, often in – to Western eyes – distant and unfamiliar places. However, it was not until the nineteenth century that plant hunting became a viable commercial undertaking, thanks in part to the rhododendron.

The rhododendron was brought to England long before then, of course – as early as the mid-seventeenth century, in fact. The renowned gardeners and plant collectors John Tradescant the Elder (1570–1638) and his son, also called John (1608–1662), described R. hirsutum in their catalogue, *Musaeum Tradescantianum*, around 1656. Eighteenth-century Quaker explorers John Bartrum (1699–1777) and Peter Collinson (1694–1768) discovered the first large-leaved rhododendron, R. maximum, and John Fraser (1750–1811) introduced R. catawbiense.

Rhododendrons reached these shores from an astonishing variety of regions. The pretty R. rhodora (now called R. canadense) came, as its modern name implies, from Canada. It features in a famous poem by the transcendentalist poet Ralph Waldo Emerson (1803–1882) and a story tells that on its trip to England, a terrible storm arose and much of the cargo was ditched overboard but not this plant, which made it safely to port. Lionel named his motor yacht *Rhodora*. Old world regions of the Caucasus and Russia contained some rhododendrons too and Vasily Pushkin (1766–1830), uncle of the famous poet and a minor poet himself, presented R. caucasicum to Kew in 1803. Joseph Hooker's landmark Himalayan expedition discovered 45 rhododendron species, which were published in the monograph *The Rhododendrons of Sikkim-Himalaya* (1849–1851).

Scottish botanist Robert Fortune (1812–1880) introduced more from China, most notably R. *fortunei* in 1855, which would later become the parent of many fine rhododendron hybrids.

The rhododendron was, therefore, not a new arrival by the early nineteenth century, but its popularity soared after the introductions of Hooker and Fortune. In fact an increasing demand for exotic plants in general led trade nurseries such as Loddiges, Lee and Kennedy and Veitch to commercialise this plant-hunting enterprise. As early as 1836 Loddiges's catalogue listed 28 varieties of R. *ponticum* and 73 Ghent azaleas, while prominent growers included the 2nd Earl of Carnarvon (1772–1833), whose Highclere Castle had 'gravel walks with long marginal belts on either side profusely studded with rhododendrons, kalmias, azaleas, vacciniums'. His was also the first private garden to become known for its rhododendron hybridisation programme: R. 'Altaclarense' is a Latinisation of 'Highclere'. There were setbacks, however. Around this time the notorious R. *ponticum* was found to be self-seeding, forming woodlands that were difficult to control. This did not, however, discourage major landowners from enriching their gardens with rhododendrons.

106 In the early twentieth century there was another explosion of interest in rhododendrons (overtaking the enormous popularity of orchids at that time) during what became the most prolific and unmatched period of plant collecting in Asia. In fact a revolution was under way around the British Isles, in gardens both commercial and private, led by the collections of plant hunters who travelled into the Sino-Himalayan areas of China, Tibet and Burma.

It is easy to see why. Several floral kingdoms come together in this region to create one of the richest areas of temperate plants. Rhododendrons and ericaceous plants can be identified here by altitude as well as by the setting of bamboo, deciduous or evergreen forest or alpine meadow. Weather conditions of rain shadow, river bed, monsoon rain or snow create an ecosystem that determines the growth pattern, habit, and the shape and size of leaf and flower.

Despite the riches it offered, this vast and complex landscape posed considerable physical challenges for travellers, facing unfamiliar terrain. Furthermore, they were sometimes – quite understandably – viewed with suspicion by those who lived there. Given the potential for failure, it is hardly surprising that garden owners who sponsored the plant hunters, directly or through syndicates, were so pleased with the results. With the new finds came significant, and often secret, hybridisation schemes, funded privately. The garden owners shared their successes at the RHS shows and the Rhododendron Society, the Rhododendron Association and the Garden Society, competing against each other with an intensity that matched that of their plant hunters in the field.

Nevertheless, one observer commented that among elite gardeners in particular there was what he called 'a curiously twisted snobbery. To have an alkaline soil in the eyes of these people, is rather like belonging to the wrong club.' Thus, despite their popularity, not all took to the Sino-Himalayan introductions, especially when a lime soil was an issue. In any case, the European mountains, along with Tasmania, Africa and North and South America also provided plenty of other possibilities for gardeners.

In addition there were some who felt that 'the multitudes of seedlings, germinating like mustard and cress from the seed sent home, rapidly transformed many British gardens into unplanned woodlands'. The commercial nurseries in particular were suspicious of the amateurs whom they felt were adversely affecting trade. This scepticism did not, however, halt the enthusiastic amateurs, who eagerly filled their own and their friends' gardens with home-made hybrids. That said, dinner party conversation may have changed for the worse: one garden writer joked, 'At one time … if you kept your ears open at a dinner party you could pick up a useful racing tip now and then; but all you hear nowadays is about the latest rhododendron or something, and the best manure to give it.'

By now plant hunters were marketers as well as hardy explorers. Photography was an essential device for promoting expeditions. Enthralling reports were sent back to sponsors and the gardening media with a view to drumming up more business. To secure the flow of clients' funds, the plant hunters sent sketches, letters and copious field notes, using a sequential numbering system to order their finds – for example, F 2440 (George Forrest's *Primula bulleyana*) and, perhaps the most famous consecutive collectors' numbers in rhododendron history, KW 7724 and KW 7225, Frank Kingdon-Ward's *Rhododendron macabeanum* and R. *elliottii* collected from Mt. Japvo

opposite · Map showing the areas explored by Forrest on his various expeditions *following pages* · see page 197

FORREST'S BOTANICAL EXPEDITIONS

On the borders of Burma, Tibet and Western China

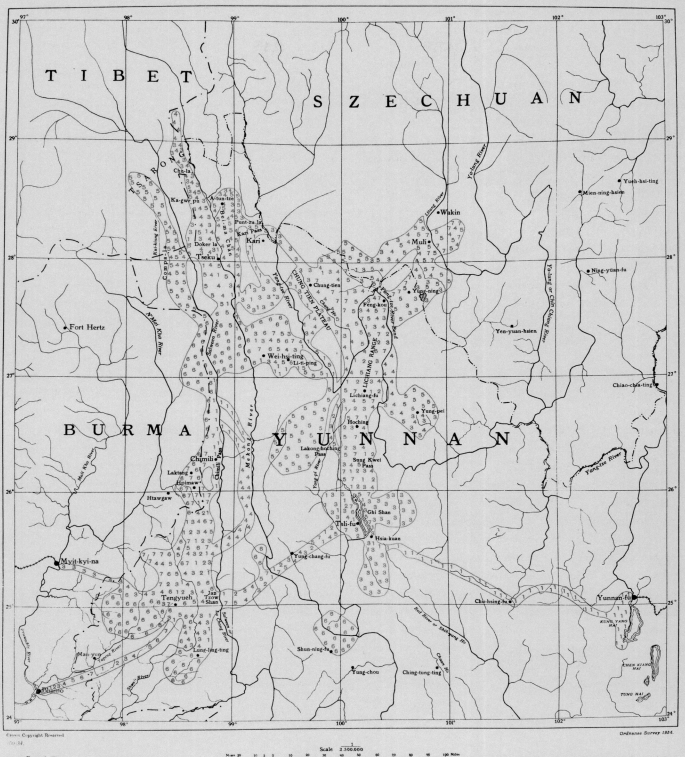

Ordnance Survey 1934.

Scale 1 : 2,500,000

Miles 20 10 5 0   10   20   30   40   50   60   70   80   90   100 Miles

Forrest's Expeditions are numbered in Red

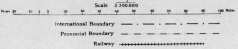

1904-6	1
1910	2
1912-14	3
1917-19	4
1921-22	5
1924-25	6
1930-31	7

International Boundary   — · — · — · — ·

Provincial Boundary   — ·· — ·· — ··

Railway   ++++++++++++++++++

Based on Survey of India maps, with the permission of the Surveyor General of India.

in the Naga Hills, north-east India in 1927. The field notes were published by the syndicates in small books easily carried in the hands of an enthusiast around his garden.

This great age of plant hunting and the fashion for collecting exotic new plants perfectly suited Exbury's acidic soil. In fact the timing of Lionel's creation at Exbury could not have been better and he eagerly supported expeditions that would help to develop it. From 1912 onwards Lionel sponsored a succession of expeditions by several plant hunters around the world. He rarely refused a request for support, but if he had not been asked to join a syndicate, he was usually able to secure seeds through his numerous contacts.

As a result of Lionel's enthusiasm and dedication, Exbury took its place as a living monument to the most outstanding plant collectors of the day and the farsighted 'amateur' who supported so many of them. During Exbury's remarkable first 20 years, the gardens received not only rhododendrons but azaleas, camellias, viburnums, cotoneasters, magnolias, primulas, heathers, acers, cherries, trees, and herbaceous and hothouse plants including orchids, nerines and hippeastrums. Lionel's boundless energy and passion for his plants and his gardens was underlined by a strong level of personal involvement that included communicating with the hunters, sharing seeds with other enthusiasts, managing syndicates, consulting Edinburgh and Kew on botanical identification, authorising expedition payments, issuing instructions on the propagation of seeds arriving at Exbury, winning awards at RHS shows and attending the horticultural committees. On top of this, he also kept up with his responsibilities at the bank.

One thing he did not do, however, was plant hunting. Some garden owners such as Lawrence Johnston (1871–1958), Reginald Cory (1871–1934) and Leonard Messel (1873–1953) journeyed with the plant hunters. Lionel was unable to abandon his responsibilities at the bank to witness for himself the native habitats of the plants that flooded into his garden. Then again, perhaps he did not need to: he was creating his own earthly paradise right there at Exbury.

To create his plant collection, Lionel engaged with the group of plant hunters at the forefront of this period of introductions – the men (in the main) who supplied the garden community with the new and exciting exotics that we take for granted in our gardens today.

One collector from whom he sought advice was Ernest Henry 'Chinese' Wilson (1876–1930), who introduced the famous

'Wilson Fifty' Kurume azaleas. Wilson's reputation for insight and commitment was well-deserved. Despite enduring much hardship during his travels, it is no exaggeration to credit Wilson with the introduction of thousands of non-native plant species to Europe and America, including *Meconopsis integrifolia*, *Clematis montana var. rubens* and *Clematis armandii*, as well as the beautiful peeling barked *Acer griseum* and, of course, Wilson's famous handkerchief tree, *Davidia involucrata*. A number of these can be found at Exbury, the largest in Home Wood, a spring flowering specimen covered with the distinctive hanging white bracts which resemble handkerchiefs; these are then followed by walnut-like fruits ripening in late autumn.

From 1917 Wilson had undertaken a systematic exploration of Korea, Formosa (Taiwan) and Japan, arriving in the town of Kurume in Japan in 1918. Here he found a great many nurseries growing rhododendron cultivars – specifically evergreen azaleas. He selected the 50 that he considered best suited to the American market both for hardiness and quality; these he sent to the Arnold Arboretum at Harvard University, but not being thought hardy they were originally grown in greenhouses outside of Boston. Two living sets were then sent to England in the early 1920s: one to J.C. Williams and the other to J.B. Stevenson at Tower Court, Ascot. Lionel, as mentioned, obtained his directly from the Yokohama Nursery in 1920. They were originally thought to be tender – and some indeed were – but most proved hardier than originally supposed; in fact a few still reside happily round the Bottom Pond in Home Wood.

While he never visited Exbury, the garden gained the benefit of Wilson's knowledge and introductions from an early stage in its development when Lionel began exchanging seeds and advice with Wilson. This continued even after Wilson's last expedition, a tour of the gardens of the world, which took place from 1920–1922 in Australia, Tasmania, New Zealand, Asia, and Africa (no one could say he was not thorough). It was after this trip that Lionel asked Wilson for tree seeds, particularly hickories, *Carya glabra*, *C. cordiformis*, *C. myristiciformis*, and *C. x laneyi*. 'I shall have the most complete collection of hickories in England. I hope they flourish at Exbury,' he wrote.

Wilson and Lionel continued to exchange seeds from plant hunters such as Joseph Rock and Frank Kingdon-Ward. The exceedingly rare *Taiwania cryptomerioides*, known as the Chinese Coffin Tree, grew in Witcher's Wood, and may have come from Wilson; the original one no longer survives but a newer

R.'Hinomayo', in Lionel's opinion the hardiest and best pink of all the Kurume azaleas

one has taken its place. As its name suggests, the aromatic and highly durable wood is valued by the Chinese for making coffins. Wilson sent four plants to the Arnold Arboretum in 1918 and seedlings to Lionel in November 1926. The first batch was disappointing but at Lionel's request Wilson sent another, better batch the next month. Wilson was also a prolific magnolia collector and gave seeds to Chenaud in Orléans to propagate, which Lionel purchased, as he was keen to collect many magnolias for Exbury.

After the death of Charles Sprague Sargent (1841–1927) Wilson was appointed his successor as Director of the Arnold Arboretum in Massachusetts. As he wrote to congratulate him,

Lionel realised that Wilson might never visit England again. Nevertheless Wilson was keen to learn how many of the plants that he had collected were still in cultivation; for example, *Rhododendron insigne* and *Staphylea holocarpa* var. *rosea* had become extremely rare. Although, as we have said, Wilson never visited Exbury, his successor, William Judd, later did, describing Exbury as being 'where rhododendrons grow like weeds'.

Alpine specialist and plant hunter Reginald Farrer (1880–1920) was the first plant hunter that Lionel sponsored directly. Called by many the 'Prince of Alpine gardeners', Farrer was successful in introducing many new alpine plants to British gardens. He was a prolific writer, publishing his most popular

R. praestans. Balf. fil.

above and opposite · Photographs taken by George Forrest

book, *My Rock Garden*, in 1907 and two volumes of *The English Rock Garden* in 1919. He was well known for his slightly overwrought language, forcefully conveying his feelings about the landscapes and flora he saw on his travels.

In 1919 Farrer embarked on a two-year plant-collecting expedition to Upper Burma. Needing sponsors, and on the advice of Isaac Bayley Balfour (1853–1922) of the Royal Botanic Garden Edinburgh, he wrote confidently to Lionel at New Court, 'I wonder if you would care to take a £100 share ... My net would sweep in everything from trees to alpines (Rhododendrons will probably bulk large): but I do not want to include the vast miscellaneous harvests of the great collectors, so shall still continue trying to send only such things as I myself have seen and judged worthy.' Impatient to begin, and needing to raise around £1,200 a season, he reminded Lionel, 'such an expedition in country so wild is inevitably bound to be a little chancy.'

On 6 November 1918, Lionel sponsored him for '£300 a year for each of the two years'. This was a watershed moment for Exbury.

Despite going to great lengths to avoid other plant hunters working in the region, Farrer had encounters with George Forrest's collectors and a sort of 'word warfare by letter and telegram' commenced between the two men. At one point Farrer came across a party of Forrest's collectors and asked Forrest to remove them. After 'two days of deliberation' Forrest wired back, '[R]egret cannot recall men'. This may not have been a bad thing – for their clients at least. William Wright Smith (1875–1956) of the Royal Botanic Garden Edinburgh wryly observed to Lionel that 'rivalry is having its effect' to 'stimulate both collectors to do their uttermost and to forward their seeds and plants with greater despatch than ever in order that they may not be forestalled'.

A total of 12 consignments of seeds returned via Edinburgh for Lionel, who worried that many of the plants Farrer sent back might not prove hardy in the British climate. Farrer too worried, 'I live sleepless till I hear of their germination. Spare no pains and no methods known to science in stimulating them to growth – a good long soak before sowing might help to wake the sleeping beauties.' Whatever methods he employed seem to have worked and, delighted by his 'beginner's luck', Lionel invested a further £700 for an equal share for himself and Kew.

Minor setbacks notwithstanding, Lionel agreed with Wright Smith on the efficiency of Farrer's collecting: 'It is pretty clear that Mr Farrer is an excellent collector of seeds, as I think the percentage of germination is exceedingly favourable.' However, from the taxonomical point of view, Wright Smith voiced a caveat: 'I am faced with the same difficulty as I have with Farrer's collections in Kansu ... he will not collect dried material of everything he sends' – highly frustrating for a herbarium-based botanist.

Lionel's input was vital to the legacy of Farrer's collecting. He worked carefully to match Farrer's numbers and notes against his Exbury seedlings so as to identify as many possible. Lionel was always eager to receive seeds of new things but he also wanted to give them the best chance so he immediately distributed them to other places too. Furthermore, he also reported back to the collectors: thus for example he wrote to Forrest in 1920, 'Your Juniper ('Coffin Tree') seeds look very promising; they have not yet come through the ground but on digging one up on Monday (the 29th) I found it had just begun to germinate. I am enclosing you a list of seeds which have come up since my last letter.'

Covered Chinese Bridge on the Shweli river showing method of
construction beneath.   Typically Tibetan.

opposite
George Forrest

right
M. insignis, grown from
seed collected by Farrer

This Coffin Tree is *Juniperus recurva* var. *coxii*, not the same as the Chinese Coffin Tree (*Taiwania cryptomerioides*) mentioned as introduced by Wilson, above: the common name is now applied to the *Taiwania* but doubtless, as Bean notes, 'several species of tree with durable, aromatic timber were used by the Chinese for making coffins'. Lionel's association with Farrer did not last long, however: tragically, Farrer became ill in the field and died on 17 October 1920. Shortly afterwards Lionel contributed an article to *The Gardeners' Chronicle* on 'Farrer's plants at Exbury'. He wrote, 'I regret that Farrer did not survive to receive our thanks and see the results of his toil.' Perhaps his finest contribution was the lovely *Magnolia insignis*, mentioned earlier, in the Winter Garden.

As Farrer had good reason to know, after his run-in with Forrest's men in Upper Burma, George Forrest (1873–1932) was at least as tenacious and committed a plant hunter as Farrer. In fact it is no exaggeration to say that the early twentieth-century woodland garden advanced enormously as a result of the introductions of George Forrest. Exbury, inevitably, was among the beneficiaries of his plant-hunting achievements. Lionel came across the Scottish plant hunter through his connections to the Royal Botanic Garden Edinburgh and J.C. Williams of Caerhays.

Forrest had made his first expedition to the north-west corner of Yunnan in 1904, sponsored by A.K. Bulley (1861–1942), a Liverpool cotton broker and owner of Bees Nursery. The trip was not short of incident: after the invasion of the Tibetan Holy City of Lhasa by the British, the Batang lamas of Tibet had risen up in rebellion attacking all outsiders, both Chinese and European; their uprising targeted Christian converts and missionaries in particular. Having abandoned his collections, Forrest fled with two elderly priests, Père Dubernard (1864–1905) and Père Bourdonnec (1859–1905), but they were both caught and murdered. Forrest hid his boots and waded through watercourses to disguise his scent; he survived for eight days on just a few ears of wheat. Eventually, after three weeks on the run, he was helped by local indigenous tribes to safety, disguised in Chinese dress.

Although he was reported missing by the Foreign Office, he soon reappeared (his family had 'mourned my loss only for a week') and, undeterred by this experience, he continued collecting, travelling with George Litton (c.1867–1906) of the British Consulate, who was mapping the region of the Salween district of Yunnan. This trip also proved life-threatening, albeit for different reasons. Forrest survived an attack of malaria; Litton did not.

Thanks to his able team of workers, Forrest returned back to England with a large hoard of plants, seeds and roots including *Lilium lankongense, Rhododendron dichroanthum* – the primary origin of the colour orange in so many modern hybrids – *Primula bulleyana* and *P. vialii*. In 1907 Forrest catalogued his herbarium at the Royal Botanic Garden Edinburgh. He also married Clementina Traill (1877–1937), a fellow Edinburgh botanist.

Forrest went out again for Bulley and J.C. Williams, collecting seeds of the compact bluish purple *R. impeditum*, *R. dichroanthum*, and *R. lacteum* from the slopes of Cangshan above Dali, which Lionel would later use extensively for hybridising at Exbury. However, Bulley and Forrest fell out dramatically and Forrest defected to the sponsorship of J.C. Williams. Frank Kingdon-Ward (1885–1958) was appointed in Forrest's place and the two plant hunters immediately became possessive over 'their' botanically rich territories.

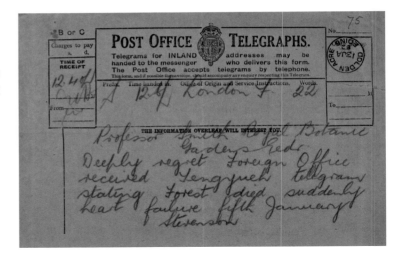

In November 1920 Forrest gave a lecture to the Rhododendron Society at Burlington House in Piccadilly. He spoke with enthusiasm about his recent expedition in China, describing it as 'but a tide of what is yet to come, not only of Rhododendrons, but of many other genera,' citing Primula and Gentiana, among others. As a new member of the Society, Lionel could not have failed to be impressed: he organised with Forrest to receive rhododendron and conifer seeds, as well as photographs and notes of the lecture, via Edinburgh. Furthermore, in 1924 when Lionel was passing through Edinburgh, possibly to visit the Sassoon estate at Tulchan, Speyside, where he had spent happy holidays as a child with his much-loved maternal aunt Lou, he went to see Forrest's dried specimens at the herbarium there. Indeed poor Wright Smith lamented the onset of rhododendronitis to Forrest, saying that he had 'had a spate of visitors, most of whom will talk of little else ... [all] more or less infected with the same virus. ... If visitors would stay away for a year something might be done.'

Lionel immediately planted the seeds supplied by Forrest at Exbury. It was not long before the network of rhododendron enthusiasts began to connect Lionel directly to Forrest. What made this tricky was that Lionel was sponsoring many plant hunters – including Forrest's main competitors, Farrer and Kingdon-Ward. This needed careful handling, not only by the plant hunters but by their sponsors too.

But Forrest could hardly be ignored by plant buyers: news of his collecting – and his daring exploits – was becoming widespread both through published articles and the plants grown by his well-known patrons. Reginald Cory, an influential horticulturalist from a shipping and coal-exporting family and a sponsor of Forrest, offered Lionel a quarter of his share of the sixth Forrest expedition of 1924–1926. Lionel wrote to the Foreign Office to arrange for an open letter of introduction for Forrest, which the Foreign Secretary, Ramsay MacDonald, approved. There was, however, a catch. The letters were accompanied with a warning that, 'there are many brigands across the Chinese frontier and that the Foreign Office will not pay any ransom towards Mr. Forrest's release.' Forrest made it safely home.

A few years later Lionel was again a sponsor of an expedition masterminded by Forrest. In 1929 he was invited to join the exclusive McLaren syndicate set up by Henry McLaren of Bodnant and Frederick Stern (1884–1967) of Highdown. This time Forrest did not travel but organised the whole expedition from Scotland, instructing his collectors to send back plants 'from the most distinctive alpine flora of Asia'. The expedition introduced species of clematis, gentian, lilium, magnolias (much to Lionel's delight), primulas, nomocharis and saxifrage. It was a resounding success, cementing Forrest's reputation not just as a great plant hunter but as one with considerable organisational skills.

Forrest's final Chinese expedition, mounted in 1930, resulted in his best haul yet. As one of the main supporters, Lionel gave £500 for Exbury with £125 on behalf of Kew. He also bought Forrest a film camera. Lionel told him he was especially interested in 'any highly coloured Magnolias' and in the case of rhododrons, 'any bright blue alpines, but they must be of the best form and colour.' After admitting, 'I am rather "teaching my grandmother to suck eggs"' he emphasised again his overriding priority: 'I do not want too many seeds but I do want seeds of what would make really good garden plants.'

On the expedition Forrest wrote to his subscribers describing some of the plants he saw in the wild, including camellias in the Shweli valley in Burma, of which he said, 'mile upon mile of the valley hillsides were absolutely covered in it … all in full and most abundant flower.' He found R. protistum var. giganteum 'at its best, in full flower, just beginning to cast thousands of trusses of huge blooms of varying shades of rose-pink to almost magenta crimson, crimson blotched at base, the ground under the trees littered inches deep with the huge fallen corollas'. Forrest announced that he 'exposed 100ft of cinefilm in the felling of our [200-year-old] specimen'. The tree he cut down was fully 90 feet high and a section cut 12 feet from the base is probably, at just over two feet wide, the largest herbarium specimen in Edinburgh, though Forrest wrote that 'it was far surpassed by others in the forest on the gully flanks where we saw specimens which must be well over 100 ft: I should say 130ft. or more.' There were other marvels. R. mackenzianum (generally now considered a synonym of R. moulmainense) 'was everywhere magnificent, up to 40–60ft laden with masses of bloom, ranging in specimens from white to the deepest crimson-magenta, with bare smooth mahogany red pillared stems'. He added, 'If we could grow that species at home as I saw it this time the enthusiasts would kneel in worship to it'. He also saw 'hundreds of most noble specimens of Rhodoleia' (which he described as 'the Hpimaw sp.' – probably Rhodoleia championii) 'in full flower, 60–90 ft.' and Michelia manipurensis (now classified as Magnolia doltsopa but this is open to doubt) '60–80 ft. in height, yellow with butter coloured blooms, scenting the air for hundreds of yards around.' What comes across is not only the extraordinary abundance of plants but also their quite exceptional size and the magic of their surroundings.

There was drama, of course. At one point, Forrest and his team experienced a severe earthquake which flung him out of his camp bed. However, Wright Smith at the Royal Botanic Garden Edinburgh confirmed that, 'the Forrest collection is without exaggeration a tremendous affair. I think I shall have between 600–700 good things to send.'

Sadly, this trip also saw Forrest's demise, though not in fact while plant hunting. Having accomplished all he had set out to achieve on the expedition, Forrest collapsed and died of heart failure while out shooting in Tengchong, Western Yunnan, in January 1932.

On hearing of the tragedy, Lionel arranged with the Foreign Office for the completion of the collecting and return of the film, lantern slides, seeds and herbarium samples to Edinburgh, and Forrest's effects to his wife. On Lionel's request, Forrest had also collected butterflies for his eldest son Eddy. Although originally mistakenly sent to the British Museum they were eventually returned, to Eddy's great delight. The Royal Botanic Garden Edinburgh received the greatest part of Forrest's herbarium material, numbering some 31,000 specimens, of which more than 5,000 were rhododendrons.

Forrest had received the Rhododendron Cup of the Royal Horticultural Society in 1930 in recognition of his discovery of 260 species of the genus, including the one named in his honour, Rhododendron forrestii. He also introduced to cultivation some of our very finest woodland garden trees and shrubs, many of which can be seen at Exbury: Rhododendron sinogrande, R. griersonianum (parent of many important red hybrids), the ground-hugging R. forrestii and Pieris formosa var. forrestii. Among perennials, there was the blue Gentiana sino-ornata, as well as Primula bulleyana and P. malacoides. Lionel arranged and paid for his burial overlooking Tengchong, but his living memorial lies in the gardens of Exbury.

above · Telegram announcing death of Forrest *below* · Joseph Rock's signature in the Exbury visitors' book

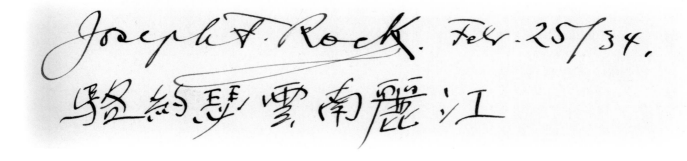

118 *above*
R. sinogrande, one of Forrest's
finest introductions

right
Plants collected by Rock
awaiting shipment, indicative
of the quantities involved

Pioneers and plant hunters · Expeditions, near and far

Lionel sponsored a number of other leading plant hunters, among them Austrian-born Joseph Rock (1884–1962). Fascinated by China from a young age, Rock taught himself Chinese by the age of 13 and was eventually fluent in many languages. He became an authority on the plants of Hawaii and curator of the herbarium, amassing more than 28,000 specimens and publishing many books on Hawaiian flora. Early in his career he collected *Hydnocarpus kurzii* from Southeast Asia, the oil from which was used at the time for treating leprosy. He also travelled extensively for the U.S. Department of Agriculture, the Arnold Arboretum and other syndicates, following in the footsteps of Augustine Henry (1857–1930), Wilson and Forrest.

As Rock's collections were held by the U.S. Department of Agriculture, they were difficult to access due to strict customs regulations. Lionel enlisted Wilson at the Arnold Arboretum to help, and after much effort obtained Rock's seeds and 1924 expedition field notes. Lionel showered praise on Rock's ability to provide viable seed in large quantities and invited him to Exbury, pronouncing, 'I think Rock is one of the best of the present collectors as all the plants that have so far flowered in my garden have proved of merit.' Obviously frustrated by the lengthy bureaucratic process, Lionel published Rock's 1925–1926 expedition field notes himself, sending Wilson a first copy.

Photography was a defining characteristic of Rock's work, which must have appealed to sponsors such as Lionel. It appealed to the even wider audience who read one of the world's best-known science and natural history publications: by publishing his articles in *The National Geographic Magazine*, Rock provided a window on a world that many of his audience would never witness.

We have already briefly mentioned Frank Kingdon-Ward, whose *Rhododendron macabeanum* and *R. elliottii* have enjoyed lasting fame. He was in fact one of the greatest explorer-plant hunters of the twentieth century. Lionel knew his work intimately, sponsoring some of his most important expeditions over a 20-year period and receiving and growing many of his iconic plants at Exbury. He published Kingdon-Ward's field notes, distributed his collections to Rhododendron Association members and through him shared the final moments of this golden age of plant hunting before war brought it to an abrupt end.

Kingdon-Ward first hunted plants in the school holidays of his teaching post at the Shanghai Public School, joining an American zoological expedition, funded by the Duke of Bedford, which travelled up the Yangtze in western China. His behaviour must have unnerved his companions at times. On one occasion he wandered off from the main party (a frequent habit of his in years to come) taking two days and nights to get back to the camp. His first book *On the Road to Tibet* was published in 1911 and he was elected a fellow of the Royal Geographical Society.

After Forrest's departure to J.C. Williams in 1911, Bulley was looking for a replacement and the 25-year-old Kingdon-Ward was recommended to him. 'Of the fine results … [he] will achieve I have no doubt.' He would expand his focus over time but on his first expedition Kingdon-Ward concentrated more on flowers – saxifrages, primulas and gentians. Even then, however, he had a way of doing things that was entirely his own.

As he became more experienced, Kingdon-Ward became a keen observer of the cycle of nature, exploring areas in spring to identify plants in flower only to return to collect seeds when the landscape had been transformed and snow covered the ground. He may have had his eccentricities, but Kingdon-Ward was, like Forrest, highly organised, with a loyal team of collectors and strategies for getting the best out of the time and resources he had, and this approach reaped its rewards. In 1922, after war service in India, he found the slipper orchid which bears his name, *Paphiopedilum wardii*.

One of the most famous of Kingdon-Ward's expeditions was to Tsangpo Gorges in 1924–1925 in the company of the young 5th Earl Cawdor (1900–1970). Lionel arranged a syndicate and the payments were made via New Court through Calcutta. Kingdon-Ward wrote of the expedition, 'Every day the scene grew more savage, the mountains were higher and steeper'. Cawdor meanwhile muttered about the food (even though they were in part provisioned by Fortnum and Mason) and in particular about Kingdon-Ward. 'It drives me clean daft to walk behind him – stopping every ten yards and hardly moving in between. … If I ever travel again, I'll make damned sure it's not with a botanist. They are always stopping to gape at weeds.'

Their most famous find was *Meconopsis baileyi*, known as the Himalayan or Tibetan blue poppy, discovered in 1886 by Père Delavay (1834–1895). Kingdon-Ward said of his first sighting, 'Suddenly I looked and there, like a blue panel dropped from heaven – a stream of blue poppies dazzling as sapphires in the pale light.' Kingdon-Ward went back in the late autumn to collect seed and *Meconopsis baileyi* was officially introduced in 1926. (It was later called *M. betonicifolia*, but the original name of *M. baileyi* has now been restored.) He found other outstanding plant species including

KW

Contents of Basket

8011. *Aeschynanthus*.
A sub-tropical epiphytic species
with large bunches of vivid
vermillion scarlet flowers.

8106. *Pleione*. A small purple
flowered rock Orchid.

8214. *Dendrobrium*. Flowers white
very fragrant. From the temperate
rain forest at 6000 ft.

8490. *Phaius or Calanthe*?
Flowers chalk white, fragrant.
A ground orchid from the forest
6000 ft. Requires deep shade.

8491 Orchid (*Dendrobrium*?)
Flowers white and purple.

He loved to camp under the stars,
swim in the snowmelt of the Yangtze
River and drink yak milk. He even ate
rhododendron flowers for the big drop
of 'honey' at the base of the corolla.

clockwise from top left
R. macabeanum; Frank Kingdon-
Ward; sample page listing plants
collected with their collector's
numbers

following page
R. macabeanum, one of
Kingdon-Ward's finest
yellow introductions

Chapter Six

Berberis tsangpoensis, Rhododendron leucaspis, R. auritum, R. venator, R. montroseanum and *R. scopulorum*. His discoveries and expedition were immortalised in his book *The Riddle of the Tsangpo Gorges*.

Lionel's share of seeds arrived at New Court via the Royal Botanic Garden Edinburgh. The highlight was one of the finest woodland primulas, KW 5781 *Primula florindae*, a giant cowslip named after Kingdon-Ward's first wife Florinda, née Norman-Thompson. (For his second wife, Jean, née Macklin, he named the rare pale bluish-pink *Lilium mackliniae*.)

Kingdon-Ward's reputation as a professional plant hunter was growing fast and in May 1926 Lionel agreed to his request to head another syndicate. By September the expedition was underway with high expectations of new discoveries of orchids, particularly cymbidiums, dendrobiums and vandas, large-leaved rhododendrons and magnolias.

Lionel continued sponsoring expeditions and receiving seeds, and then distributing them or growing them at Exbury. In the Rhododendron House that he used for his tender rhododendrons he had success with KW 3776, *R. pachypodum*, and KW 6333 *R. nuttalli* var. *stellatum*, with its apple-green starry calyx. Kingdon-Ward's plants in cultivation were showing wonderful results. 'Every year new pleasures are delighting the eyes of those who have waited anxiously to see the results of their labours,' as Lionel put it. However, Lionel's letters also had firm instructions to 'only collect new plants', as the huge quantities were becoming almost unmanageable. As head of the syndicate, Lionel published Kingdon-Ward's field notes from the 1927–1928 expedition. He was by now in close communication with Kingdon-Ward, his favourite plant hunter, who regularly dropped in for lunch at New Court to discuss the seed numbers and plant descriptions or at Exbury to see his seedlings 'looking very healthy'.

Lionel sponsored three more of Kingdon-Ward's expeditions in the 1930s. His 1933–1934 expedition in particular confirmed that plant hunting had become a marketable operation. Kingdon-Ward had acquired an agent, Buchanan, and issued a promotional pamphlet, *Plant-hunting Expedition to Mysterious Tibet*, for new subscribers, with his logo proudly displayed. The pamphlet promised a handbook, field notes and personal letters from the great man himself to subscribers. Business was brisk. Lionel advised Kingdon-Ward to collect large quantities of identified seed for new subscribers, and to only collect species for the key syndicate members, in order to get as much of a commercial gain as possible from Kingdon-Ward's time. Field notes were published at 7/6d a copy from New Court, with 175 applications.

In 1934 Kingdon-Ward wrote to Lionel about an expedition over the Patkoi mountains between Assam and Burma to ascend heights 'which exceed 10,000 feet'. This time the collections would be divided into plant groups, the most expensive being 'Group C rhododendrons at 7 & 5 guineas'. As the largest sponsor of the 1937–1938 expedition to North Burma, Lionel distributed large quantities of seed to the Americans and to Rhododendron Association members from a catalogue that Kingdon-Ward had compiled, alongside seeds from Exbury's plants at five shillings a packet.

As the 1930s came to an end geopolitics began to intrude on the plant-hunting business. Kingdon-Ward acknowledged that his travels 'sooner or later must be affected by events of such far-reaching importance' and funding was stalling. The American Vernay-Cutting expedition from November 1938 to April 1939 to the Hpimaw and Htawgaw Hills of Northern Burma was the last expedition Lionel sponsored. The second year of the expedition went undersubscribed by the English. For one thing, there was new competition in the field. Chinese botanists headed by the female expert Professor Shiu-Ying Hu (1910–2012) were collecting for the RHS and leading the establishment of plant science in China. At the same time visits by outsiders were increasingly difficult and what had once merely been a border that was tricky to access was now becoming politically impenetrable. Then the Japanese invaded. Kingdon-Ward's intimate knowledge of the terrain meant he had little trouble in escaping into India from Burma, but plant hunting in the area was no longer an option for him and many others.

He had, however, achieved an extraordinary amount, for which we can all be grateful. He had a particular affinity for yellow, thus *R. macabeanum*, mentioned earlier, and *R. wardii*, named after him. His contribution to the range of plants at Exbury and his close relationship with his long-standing sponsor, Lionel, were unique: it is to the benefit of garden-lovers today that both these remarkable men spent so much of their lives searching for the ultimate plant collection.

Lionel also sponsored plant hunters on other continents. One of them, Harold Comber (1897–1969), was a talented gardener and plant hunter whom he took under his wing. Comber's father James (1866–1953) was the head gardener at Nymans, West Sussex, owned by the Messels, a stockbroking family of German Jewish origin.

123

Comber was chosen for two expeditions that Lionel sponsored. The Andes syndicate (1925–1926) was led by Henry McLaren of Bodnant and Lionel was the second largest sponsor. To ease the journey he provided references through the Rothschild bank with the Chilean consul in Argentina and organised the personal accident insurance through his directorship of the Alliance Assurance Company. A prudent move perhaps, but Comber returned unscathed and sent back seeds and herbarium specimens of over 1,200 species – *Nothofagus antarctica*, *Embothrium coccineum*, *Berberis montana* and *B. comberi*, among many others, including of course eucryphias – Nymans had been responsible for the famous *Eucryphia* x *nymansensis* 'Nymansay' (the name comes from the better of two seedlings designated 'Nymans A' and 'Nymans B'). The expedition was so well organised that the syndicate got a refund. A surprised Lionel wrote to McLaren, 'I think you are a much better manager than I am, as I never have anything back from my expeditions.'

At the final meeting of the Andes syndicate, Lionel asked Comber whether he would consider a trip to Tasmania. Keen to explore an area that was botanically less well known to him – and against advice from the Royal Botanic Garden Edinburgh and Kew – Lionel put out a circular to potential sponsors in July 1929. Tree ferns from Tasmania were the main attraction and much of what Comber collected was not new to science. Comber wanted to publish 'with new and revived specific names' but had to wait till they had been 'authenticated by publication in the Kew Bulletin, or else they will be treated as old synonyms and sunk afresh'. In spite of some scepticism from syndicate members, such as Colonel Stephenson Clarke (1862–1948) of Borde Hill, Sussex, in September 1930 thirty tree ferns arrived at Exbury from Tasmania. Miss Milburn, Lionel's secretary, arranged their distribution by train around the country to the satisfied members of the syndicate.

In addition to his devotion to the exclusive world of plant hunting and his sponsorship of it, Lionel took a considerable interest in what horticulture could do for the wider community, as we shall see in the following chapter.

above
R. protistum var. *giganteum*, initially discovered by Forrest but also collected by Kingdon-Ward

opposite · Rhododendrons, *see page 196*

Leading a horticultural movement

INNOVATION AT EXBURY

CHAPTER 7

A strong sense of community was a given for the family; Lionel was no exception to this tradition, especially when it came to horticulture.

Lionel was always looking for ways to support and nurture the 'hobby' that was his passion, sharing his plants in endless exchanges, not only in Britain but around the world.

He saw himself as a link between amateur, botanist and trade, presenting himself as having the 'idle curiosity of an amateur', yet knowing full well that his knowledge was greater than most when it came to rhododendrons due to the scale of his collection and the intensity of his hybridising. He believed that the pooling of plant knowledge within the wider horticultural community, both amateur and professional, would be of huge benefit to all – and he wanted to set an example.

Given the level of debate in horticulture this was a positive approach at a time when arguments between botanists and gardeners led to fierce disagreements on plant identification and kept the gentleman gardeners busy at their writing desks. A key problem was taxonomy: the flood of rhododendrons in the early part of the century, already alluded to, meant order was needed. By a stroke of luck – or possibly genius – the botanist Sir Isaac Bayley Balfour of the Royal Botanic Garden Edinburgh hurriedly erected a taxonomic 'dam', dividing rhododendrons into series by arranging them in groups of similar appearance. This was meant to be temporary and flexible – an extensive range of pigeonholes into which new discoveries could be posted – but proved so popular with gardeners that it soon became codified into a system. While Balfour's approach no longer guides

taxonomy, newer scientific revisions of the genus have retained some of its virtues by imitating the approach of dividing the plant types into sections and subsections.

Despite his status as an amateur, Lionel always recognised the value of applying scientific and botanical rigour to gardening. For instance, since the fifteenth century the idea of flattening and storing dry specimens of plants in a herbarium had been adopted as a reference for the known plant kingdom in both private and state-held collections. With this in mind, in 1919 Lionel and A.K. Bulley purchased the herbarium of the famous French botanist (and clergyman) Hector Léveillé (1864–1918) much to the chagrin of the Americans who had bid for it too. They presented it to the Royal Botanic Garden Edinburgh to help them identify the species' names from Léveillé's detailed herbarium notes.

It is in some part due to Lionel's persistence and endeavour that the plant hunters' discoveries – and the subsequent species, varieties and hybrids – were documented at all. Early volumes, such as Millais's great two-volume *Rhododendrons and the Various Hybrids* (published in 1917 and 1924), had tackled the subject, but the genus had moved on at a rapid pace. Lionel promoted the importance of the classification of rhododendrons to encourage growers to list their plants in cultivation, like those at Exbury, and send them to the Royal Botanic Garden Edinburgh for recording. He felt that this was the only way to quantify what

above · Lionel (centre) and guests in the Glade opposite · Lionel's card index for R. cinnabarinum, with flowering dates noted previous pages · see page 197

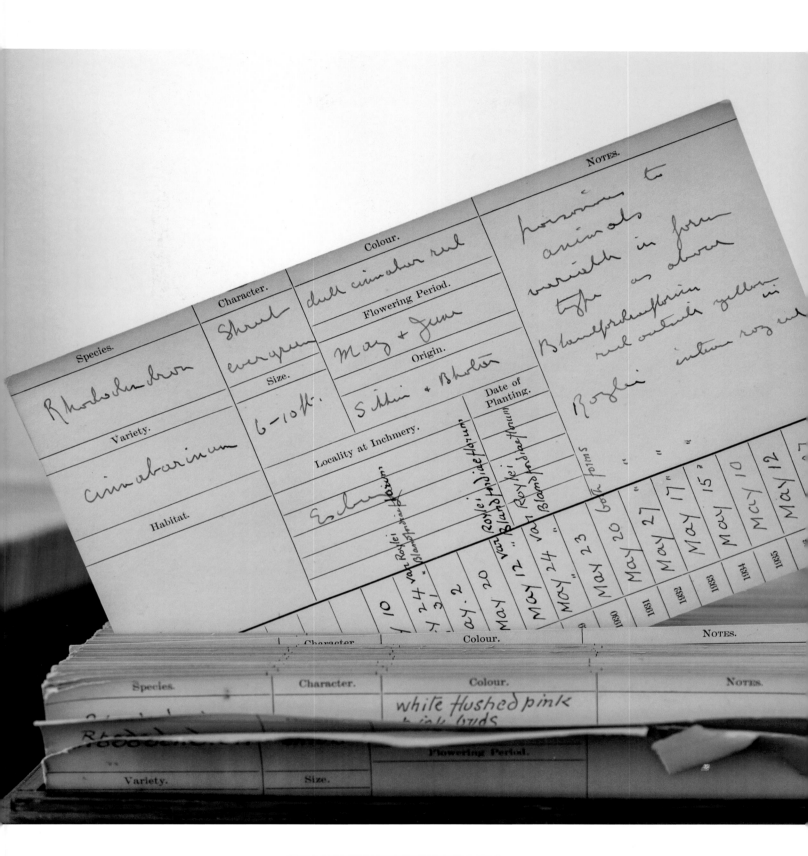

had been grown from the plant hunters' collections. In return he gained a valuable overview of contemporary advances in rhododendron cultivation for Exbury.

It was perhaps in this spirit of constructive endeavour that a succession of garden visits occurred throughout the flowering season, allowing fellow gardeners to check up on propagation trials and perhaps take home some seed or pollen. Likewise when he visited elsewhere he hoped to exchange things: thus he wrote to Farrer that he was 'just off to Cornwall for the Easter holidays where, by offering some of the seedlings that I am raising from your seeds, I hope to acquire many treasures for my own garden'.

Visitors from private gardens and horticultural institutions were invited down to Exbury to see the impressive quantities of stock and, encouraged by Lionel, to make lists of what they wanted for their own garden or nursery. He purchased innumerable plants for Exbury, which he readily shared with his fellow enthusiasts. He was particularly keen to encourage younger gardeners: Sir John Carew Pole (1902–1993) returned to his home at Antony in Cornwall after a weekend only to be rung by the stationmaster informing him that Lionel had sent him a wagonload of rhododendrons. Lionel was always a generous donor of plants, to friends, visitors, members of the royal family,

universities, charities and children's homes. By letter, at RHS Flower Shows, and during lunches at New Court, Rhododendron Association and Garden Society meetings, visits to private and botanic gardens and holidays abroad, Lionel championed the horticultural cause.

As the number of enthusiasts swelled, Lionel became concerned at the limited nature of the Rhododendron Society; a moderniser at heart, he was a chief negotiator in its 1925 discussions about opening the membership to a wider audience. It took some time for the old guard to come round. Finally, in 1928 a new organisation, the Rhododendron Association, was established, with Lionel as President. This new body, unlike the Rhododendron Society, was open to all who wished to join, be they amateur or professional. It boasted a membership of over 600 at the end of its first three years, quite a few of them from the more restrictive Rhododendron Society. King George VI agreed to be a patron, sealing the Association's authority within the horticultural world.

Lionel had won the argument for the modernisers: now the work began. On joining, new members received the latest *Year Book of the Rhododendron Association* (published from 1929–1939): these were a mine of information, listing species, hybrids, what

crosses had produced what (singularly useful) and collectors' numbers. Lionel also contributed a series of articles on all the species, together with some notes on hybrids. Occasionally he showed a flash of self-deprecating humour, as when he commented, 'not worth growing except for the rhododendron maniac who wants to have one of every species – I have it at Exbury, but one plant is enough.' J.B. Stevenson's masterful *The Species of Rhododendron*, published by the Rhododendron Society in 1930, also set things on a more professional footing. All this brought the rhododendron and its classification into the wider gardening community for the benefit of everyone.

Lionel's proposal in 1930 to hold the first joint RHS and Rhododendron Association trials at Exbury might have been a touch self-serving, but applying stringent standards was instinctive to his hybridiser's eye, and the offer would give opportunities for varietal quality control across the whole rhododendron community. Requests were made to the leading growers, including Walter Slocock Ltd., R. Wallace, J. Cheal and Sons, Harry White's, Russells and Waterers, to send one plant of each of their best hybrid rhododendrons and azaleas raised since 1918 to be planted in the Exbury trial ground at the north of the gardens at the Top Nursery.

The first meeting, on Saturday 29 April 1933, took place, rather conveniently, during an Exbury gardening weekend. A Joint Exbury Trials Committee, composed of RHS and Rhododendron Association members, inspected the plants in situ and made recommendations for RHS awards. The Association *Year Book* was used for reference and name clashes were dealt with firmly. A number of RHS awards – an FCC (First Class Certificate) and fourteen AMs (Awards of Merit) – were proposed after the committee's visit. The following year invitations were extended to allow submissions from Dutch nurseries.

The Rhododendron Association attempted to keep the Exbury trials going, but the combined problems of frost damage and the packed diaries of the judges may have led Lionel to realise that the operation would be better off in RHS hands. In 1938 he agreed that the trials be relocated to RHS Garden Wisley in Surrey, at a site to the west of Battleston Hill. The new trial ground needed to be prepared before the Exbury lorry arrived with its precious cargo – and was, much to the relief of Lionel and his head gardener. The RHS formally thanked Lionel 'for his kindness in arranging these trials and growing the plants at

opposite · R. Carita Group   above · R. augustinii

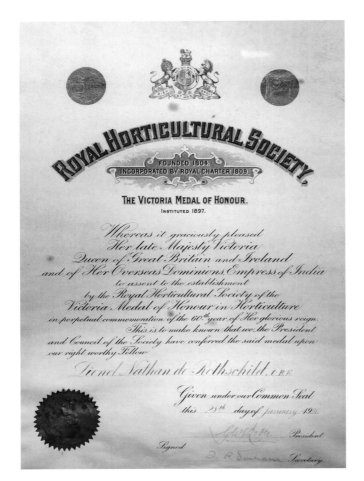

this page
Lionel's Victoria Medal of
Honour; letter from Euan Cox,
fellow woodland gardener and
editor of *The New Flora and Silva*

opposite · View Point

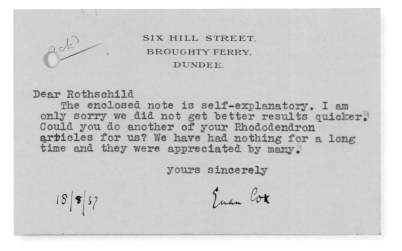

SIX HILL STREET,
BROUGHTY FERRY,
DUNDEE.

Dear Rothschild
The enclosed note is self-explanatory. I am
only sorry we did not get better results quicker.
Could you do another of your Rhododendron
articles for us? We have had nothing for a long
time and they were appreciated by many.

yours sincerely

18/8/37

Euan Cox

Exbury during the past few years'. The trials are also part of his horticultural legacy: they continue today, overseen by the RHS Woody Plant Trials Sub-Committee. Much of the valuable work of the RHS was achieved through numerous committees composed of professional and enthusiast alike. Lionel was a good committee man, bringing people together, proposing new ideas, smoothing over arguments. Always enthusiastic, he was a keen participant in all the shows, putting plant after plant from Exbury up for awards (and winning many of them).

He also played his part behind the scenes. In 1924 it was agreed that the RHS-owned Exhibition Hall, known as the Lindley Hall, at Vincent Square (which had originally been part-financed by Lionel's uncle, Alfred) was becoming far too crowded during the weekly shows. Lionel was the natural choice to lead the 'New Hall' Financing Committee. To great approval the 'New Hall', in Greycoat Street, Westminster, was successfully opened, within budget, in 1928; it is now known as the Lawrence Hall.

In recognition of his contribution to the world of horticulture, particularly through his devotion to rhododendrons and orchids, Lionel received the prestigious RHS Victoria Medal of Honour in 1930. He was in good company: other holders of the award included Sir Joseph Hooker, Gertrude Jekyll, Frederick Sander the 'Orchid King' (1847–1920), Lionel's cousin the naturalist Walter Rothschild of Tring Park and James Hudson (Lionel's Gunnersbury mentor).

Lionel promoted rhododendrons through his own writing too. He was a prolific contributor to the gardening press, submitting comments, arguing the provenance of certain plants or simply describing the plants growing at Exbury. His interest in the horticultural press even led to him chairing a syndicate to save one of the greatest gardening publications of the day, *Curtis's Botanical Magazine*.

Founded by William Curtis (1746–1799), an apothecary and botanist at Kew, in 1787, the magazine had been edited by William Hooker (1785–1865) and by his son, Joseph. It was, and remains today, the pride of the horticultural community, the oldest illustrated periodical in the world devoted to plants. However, in 1920 copyright-holders and publishers Messrs. Lovell Reeve and Co. decided it was no longer commercially viable. There was a rumour that the copyright was likely to pass to an owner in the United States.

The Gardeners' Chronicle believed that if production ceased, 'the event would be a disaster to horticulture all over the world, and

would undoubtedly diminish the prestige of British Horticulture'. Lionel agreed and in 1921, Lionel, Reginald Cory and Henry Elwes (1846–1922) took urgent action: the copyright was acquired for £250. They then offered it to Kew, hoping that the Ministry of Agriculture, which was then responsible for Kew, would fund continued publication. The Ministry turned them down.

Recognising the importance of the magazine and its significance to botanists and gardeners alike, they then presented the copyright and goodwill to the RHS, which bought the old stock and resumed publication in 1922. Henry Elwes has always been cited as the key mover in the rescue and Reginald Cory paid for the missing 1921 volume – the so-called 'Cory volume', which appeared in 1938. The illustrious magazine, now appearing with hand-coloured plates by the talented botanical artist Lillian Snelling (1879–1972), was saved by these three men and continues to this day.

Later in the same decade a new horticultural magazine appeared, *The New Flora and Silva*. Its first number, in 1928, was edited by Euan Cox (1893–1977), owner of a famous woodland garden (Glendoick Gardens in Perthshire) and an experienced plant hunter, who had travelled with Farrer. Over the years Lionel contributed many excellent articles to the magazine such as 'Some New Rhododendrons of Quality', 'On Hybrid Rhododendrons' and 'Rhododendron Notes'. Financial strains were never far away, however, and in 1937 Cox turned to Lionel for help.

While Lionel contributed £200 to the small company set up to purchase the magazine, other offers were not so generous and a year later a syndicate led by Dulau, the publishers, took control. The admired gardener and watercolour painter Lady Beatrix Stanley (1877–1944) became the editor and Cox moved on. *The New Flora and Silva* had only lasted ten years under Cox, in which time it carried some of Lionel's best writing about his gardens at Exbury. Only one more edition was produced; publication ceased on the declaration of war.

Lionel also found an outlet for his horticultural enthusiasm in the Garden Society, started in 1920. This was, and remains, a small group of people who are passionate about their gardens and plants, all of whom were originally RHS Fellows. Meeting twice a year over dinner, members produced plants, in particular of new introductions, and of interest to the others. Dinners coincided with the first day of the RHS meetings. The society's motto, *Petimus Damusque Vicissim*, translated as 'Turn by turn we ask and give', conveys the mutual respect felt between these gentleman gardeners.

133

Leading a horticultural movement · Innovation at Exbury

Lionel's horticultural knowledge could sometimes be called upon in more unusual ways: this – and his continuing love of motoring – led him to take a significant part in a government initiative, the Ministry of Transport's Roads Beautifying Association (RBA).

The purpose of the RBA – to mix function with aesthetics – was forward-thinking for its time. After the Roads Improvement Act of 1925, local authorities were empowered to acquire highway marginal land along the new roads for the purposes of landscaping. Their initial attempts were unsuccessful and expert horticultural guidance was urgently sought.

The RBA was based on the US Department of Agriculture's successful model, with annual subscriptions from organisations such as the Royal Automobile Club and the Cement and Concrete Association. The Duchess of York was its early Patron and Dr Wilfrid Fox (1875–1962), owner of Winkworth Arboretum, was appointed the Honorary Secretary. Lionel chaired the Technical Sub-Committee and volunteered his expert knowledge of ornamental planting schemes from Exbury which, in the committee's view, would greatly enhance the landscaping of the new roads. He also visited sites and compiled detailed reports.

Advisory booklets were published, such as *Practical Instruction for the Planting of Roadside Trees and Shrubs*, *Advice on Pruning of Roadside and Street Trees* and *Standard Specifications for Trees and Shrubs for Roadside Planting*. There was even a calendar with colour photographs of English scenes of new roads, which was sold at Christmas.

As for its work on the roads themselves, the Association had some innovative ideas such as planting white-stemmed silver birch *Betula jacquemontii* on corner bends to reflect the lights of an approaching car or planting poplars to denote a crossroads. Fast-growing evergreens on the central reservation would, it suggested, create an anti-dazzle screen. Similarly, the purple colour of flowering cherries was held not to distract the driver's eyes, making cherry trees both attractive and safe for roadside planting. In fact tree planting in general would be aesthetically useful, the Association argued, hiding the new roads from beauty spots in the surrounding countryside.

As local Branch President, Lionel checked on the progress of relevant projects, such as the screening of the Esso Petroleum oil refinery at Fawley, on his drive home to Exbury. He also visited the controversial sites of the Winchester and Totton bypasses in 1940 to review the planting plans provided by Hillier's nurseries, which included berberis, ilex, mahonia and the cotoneaster hybrids C.'Saint Monica' and C.'Cornubia'. The highly decorative scheme did, however, raise concerns from some commentators about planting non-native ornamental garden plants such as these in a rural setting. To them, it appeared incongruous and the economics of maintenance unfeasible.

One might, of course, raise an eyebrow at Lionel's idealistic example of the beautiful mile-long drive at Caerhays lined with rhododendrons and flowering cherries. Certainly Wilfred Fox had to politely reign in Lionel's enthusiasm for the use of rhododendrons and azaleas, which grew happily in the dappled, moist shade of Exbury but not in the hot, dry and exposed environment of a dual carriageway.

Plans and publications from The Roads Beautifying Association

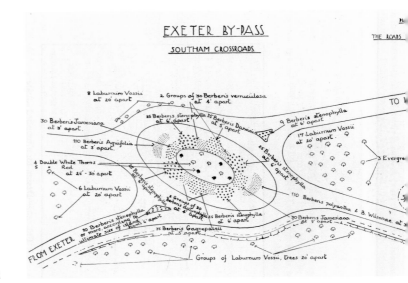

THE ROADS BEAUTIFYING ASSOCIATION

PATRONESS :
HER MAJESTY THE QUEEN.

President :
Col. The Rt. Hon. The Lord Mount Temple, P.C.

Vice-Presidents :

The Rt. Hon. The Earl of Crawford and Balcarres, K.T., P.C., F.R.S.
Sir Edward Holland.
The Rt. Hon. Lord Aberconway, C.B.E., F.L.S., V.M.H.
Col. Sir Francis Younghusband, K.C.S.I., K.C.I.E.
The Lady Leconfield.
The Rt. Hon. Herbert Morrison.
The Rt. Hon. E. L. Burgin, M.P.

Chairman of the Executive Committee :
The Rt. Hon. Lord Clinton, P.C., G.C.V.O.

Chairman of the Technical Sub-Committee :
L. de Rothschild, Esq., O.B.E., V.M.H.

Chairman of the Finance and Propaganda Sub-Committee :
The Rt. Hon. Lord Farrer.

Deputy-Chairman :
Sir Arthur Hill, K.C.M.G., F.R.S., V.M.H.

Deputy-Chairman :
F. R. S. Balfour, Esq., F.L.S., V.M.H.

Deputy-Chairman :
Major F. C. Stern, O.B.E., M.C., F.L.S.

Hon. Treasurer :
A. J. WALEY, Esq

Hon. Secretary :
WILFRID FOX, Esq., M.D., F.R.C.P.
Telephone : SLOANE 9050.

HORTICULTURAL ADVISER :
W. J. BEAN, Esq., C.V.O., V.M.H.

7, BUCKINGHAM PALACE
GARDENS, S.W.1

THE Roads Beautifying Association exists to promote the planting and beautifying of the new highways of this country, and for this purpose experts from Kew, the Royal Horticultural Society, Government Forestry Departments, and owners of the leading gardens of England have formed themselves into the voluntary central body of the Association, and give their services in inspecting, mile by mile, the many new and widened roads all over Great Britain. As a result of their work the great arterial roads out of London and the big Cities are being planted with trees suited to their climate and soil conditions, and adding year by year a growing natural beauty to their surroundings. Roadside conditions are the most difficult of all for young trees, and those with skilled and intimate knowledge of horticulture are in the best position to advise, and to safeguard local authorities from paying money for inferior, unsuitable stock which will never thrive, or form in years to come the noble trees which we associate with our English landscape. It is probable that with dwindling private planting, following the effect of taxation upon the tenure of land in these days, roadside trees are destined to make the most permanent mark upon the landscape of our time. We ask most earnestly for your financial support and co-operation.

WHAT WE HAVE DONE

At the request of the County Councils and other authorities conce[...] for the following :—

BUCKINGHAMSHIRE
Aylesbury-Uxbridge Road
Beaconsfield Parkway (London-Oxford Road)
North Orbital Road

CAERNARVONSHIRE
Griffiths Crossing Improvement

CARMARTHENSHIRE
Trunk Road No. 10, Carmarthen Bridge

CHESHIRE
Shotwick-Frodsham Road (10 miles)

CORNWALL
Penzance-Hayle Road

DENBIGHSHIRE
Wrexham-Ruabon Road

DERBYSHIRE
Chesterfield-Chapel-en-le-Frith Road
Chesterfield-Derby Road at Tupton

DEVONSHIRE
Exeter By-Pass

DURHAM
New Park at Jarrow

ESSEX
Colchester By-Pass
Lea Valley Arterial Road at Chingford

GLAMORGANSHIRE
Porthcawl U.D.C. Roads
South Wales and Monmouthshire Trading Estate

GLOUCESTERSHIRE
Filton By-Pass
Stratford Road, Stroud

HAMPSHIRE
Basingstoke By-Pass
Havant Road

HAMPSHIRE (Continued)
Ringwood By-Pass
Romsey By-Pass
Southampton New Docks
Sutton-Scotney By-Pass
Titchfield By-Pass
Wickham Square
Winchester By-Pass

HERTFORDSHIRE
Bonar Law College, Ashridge Park
North Orbital Road
Rickmansworth By-Pass

KENT
Coastal Road
Harrietsham By-Pass
Sidcup By-Pass

LANCASHIRE
Dunnings Bridge-Litherland Road
Liverpool-East Lancashire Road

LEICESTERSHIRE
Abbey Lane and Loughborough R[...]
Earl Shilton By-Pass
Market Harborough By-Pass
Market Harborough Public Park
Melton Road Improvement Schem[...]

MIDDLESEX
Bounds Green Road, Wood Green

NORTHAMPTONSHIRE
Silverstone By-Pass

OXFORDSHIRE
Oxford-Henley Road, Bix Impro[...] ment

SHROPSHIRE
Shrewsbury By-Pass

SOMERSET
Taunton Street Planting

The
ROADS BEAUTIFYING ASSOCIATION
ANNUAL REPORT
1936-1937

Photo: J. Dixon Scott.

7 BUCKINGHAM PALACE
GARDENS, LONDON, S.W.1

135

Leading a horticultural movement · Innovation at Exbury

In the end Exbury and Knap Hill found more appropriate uses for their plants, supplying them for philanthropic projects such as the Bournville Village Trust and the Jewish Youth Camp.

By the time that the Trunk Roads Act was passed in 1937 and 4,500 miles of trunk roads were transferred to Ministry of Transport control, approximately 40 schemes had been designed by the RBA. In 1938 the landscape architect Geoffrey Jellicoe (1900–1996) spoke at an RBA meeting on the value of design in the planting of central reservations and roundabouts. By 1941 a total of 28 councils in England had taken the advice of the Association and over 400 miles of carriageway and roadside had been planted.

By 1938, however, while Jellicoe was extolling the virtues of design in highway planting, there were also signs that the country was now preparing for war and economic hardship was touching all areas of public investment. Wilfred Fox was dismissed, the grant retracted and the Ministry moved its activities internally. At the same time Lionel's health worsened and the Exbury connections dissolved.

The association itself was disbanded in 1949. Its members had shared their expert horticultural knowledge to be a catalyst for change and, as an article in the *Journal of the Royal Horticultural Society* put it, 'you may not always agree with the Roads Beautifying Association, but they do know what will grow'. The standards set by the Association in beautifying roads and highways for the enjoyment of all users were high, even if they have sometimes been more honoured in the breach than the observance.

clockwise from top · Royal visits to Exbury: Edward, Prince of Wales, greeted by Mariloo in 1934; Queen Mary's visit in 1925

previous pages · see page 197

EXBURY & THE ROYAL FAMILY

During the 1930s the country experienced a number of major royal events in rapid succession: a jubilee, and two coronations, each of which was attended by commemorative events, sometimes involving a horticultural element in which Lionel played a part.

What are believed to be his only surviving drawings for a planting plan – a fruiting cherry orchard for Frogmore House – are associated with this period. Lionel sat on the Windsor Park Consultative Committee at the invitation of Sir John Stirling-Maxwell, 10th Baronet, of Pollok (1866–1956), a Scottish politician and one of the founding members of the National Trust for Scotland. A keen gardener and fellow rhododendron enthusiast, Stirling-Maxwell had exchanged seeds and received hybrids from Exbury. Lionel knew Windsor Park from childhood, when his uncle Arthur Sassoon (1840–1912) had rented a house there from time to time.

The members of the committee, which included the owner of Dawyck, F.R.S. Balfour (1873–1945), W.J. Bean, and Eric Savill (1895–1980) of Windsor, met regularly at Frogmore House to consider the tree planting. The removal of unsightly conifers and their replacement with new oaks was specified for the Long Walk. Lionel's plan for a fruiting cherry orchard between Frogmore House and the kitchen garden, with wisteria and laburnum along the paths seemed to the royal family to be 'a delightful idea'.

In 1937 the committee helped in the planning of a grove of oaks to commemorate the Coronation, close to the Prince Consort's Plantation, which was renamed as the King George VI Coronation Plantation. The plan was for twenty different species of oak to be planted 'in such a way as to conform as much as possible to the points of a compass of the territories of the British Isles'. This was a fitting commemoration for a new monarch, particularly for one who was such a keen gardener. While tree planting had been a frequent royal pastime, there had never been such a large-scale tree-planting scheme involving Windsor Great Park and the Commonwealth.

On 19 June 1937 King George VI, accompanied by Queen Elizabeth, planted the first oak, followed by representatives from the British territories, watched quietly by Lionel and Mariloo. Sir Eric Savill (he was knighted in 1955) became Keeper of the Gardens and created The Savill Garden, a particular home for rhododendrons and azaleas. It is testament to how well they got on that after Lionel's death, Mariloo sent many rhododendrons there to safeguard their future.

However, the celebrations occasioned by the Coronation were soon to be dampened by the coming of war and Exbury would be directly affected by both wartime restrictions and enemy bombing. The early 1940s also saw Exbury face a different challenge: the loss of the man who did so much for the gardens in particular and horticulture in general.

Exbury's
National Service

YEARS OF TURMOIL AND CHANGE

CHAPTER 8

'With the death of Lionel de Rothschild, English horticulture in general, and the rhododendron world in particular, have lost one of their most devoted servants and an acknowledged master.' *Country Life*, February 1942

opposite · Lionel enjoying a cigar while mountain-climbing on a European holiday *previous pages* · *see page 197*

Members of the Rothschild family living in Europe had experienced the brutal rise of the Nazis long before the outbreak of war on 1 September 1939. From 1938 onwards, many left the countries that had been their home for generations. In a sad coda to the story of the family's earliest horticultural endeavours, the original garden of Amschel von Rothschild's house in Frankfurt was destroyed in an Allied bombing raid towards the end of the war.

The first few months of war were uneventful within the New Forest area, but events soon moved more swiftly. In May and June 1940 the nation waited nervously for news of the evacuation of 330,000 Allied soldiers from Dunkirk. Then, in November 1940, the war came much closer to home for the residents of Exbury when the bombing of Southampton began. The Southampton Blitz lasted until July 1941; the ground shuddered and the glow of the burning city could be seen from miles away.

At one point Exbury village temporarily housed some of the refugees; Lionel offered Exbury House on a more permanent basis but it was felt to be too near Southampton for safety. Instead the park was lit with flares to distract enemy planes – and bombs landed frequently at Exbury. Home Wood got a direct hit – 'one crater 56 feet across' – as did the park.

The glasshouses also suffered, and the Rhododendron House was shattered. Lionel reported, 'I am afraid my Rhododendron House is done in, so is the Clivia house … I had one bomb 20 yards from the backdoor right in the middle of a clump of ponticum … where the incendiaries have only burnt some of the foliage. I will cut this off and see if they will grow again.' But he remained boldly optimistic, remarking, 'It is fortunate that the Germans are poor shots.'

The bombing continued long after the main Blitz was called off. William Rattue the gamekeeper wrote regularly to Eddy, who served in France, North Africa and Italy, throughout the war. In July 1943, Rattue described how a bomb – 'a fine big fat fellow he was' – had landed at Exbury near the petrol pump and was being dug out.

If it had gone off, he said, it 'would have lifted the garages over the house and the house would have had a pretty bad shaking-up'.

Not just bombing but the changing priorities wartime demanded were now a concern for gardeners. While the government's 'Dig for Victory' campaign – encouraging vegetable, fruit and herb growing in private gardens or public spaces – undoubtedly had a higher profile, the RHS also published useful advice to wartime gardeners. In 1939 it published an article entitled, 'The Garden in War-Time' in which it noted that '[t]he national demands entail the deflection of much labour from its normal course', as the young men of the villages were called up for service and gardening staff reduced to those retainers too old to go to war. The RHS still had high expectations (this being the beginning of the war, before rationing and mobilisation really came into effect): 'It is clearly the duty of all owners and cultivators of gardens, whilst exercising every economy, to maintain their gardens as efficiently as circumstances will allow.' For a garden as large as Exbury, the stern advice of the RHS on turfing over flower beds, holding back on watering, no unnecessary pruning, mowing grass only near the house and certainly not rolling the lawns was understandable, but perhaps sadder for Lionel was their instruction that '[t]he seed pods of Azaleas, Rhododendrons, Laburnums, etc., should remain unpicked. The flowering in the following year may be reduced but much labour will be saved.' While the phrasing is archaic, the sentiment still resonates in current times: 'The establishment of the garden and the plants in it represent the investment of capital which, so long as it is cared for, returns interest in the form of refreshment to the spirit of man, and to vast numbers the purest of human pleasures: refreshment and pleasure more necessary in times of stress than at any other.'

Lionel would have whole-heartedly agreed but by this time, however, he was seriously unwell. His health started to deteriorate in the autumn of 1940. The prognosis was not good.

left
View of the Beaulieu River and
the marshes along River Walk

opposite
Autumn colours, *see page 196*

144

He was suffering from lung cancer and towards the end he was
confined to his room. His daughter Rosemary, on leave from
her wartime role in the X-ray department of a London hospital,
visited him at Exbury to see her once energetic father weakened
by the harsh medicines of a hopeless cancer treatment. Lionel
died peacefully on 28 January 1942 in London, his devoted wife
Mariloo beside him.

Eulogies at his death celebrated the exceptional place he
held in British gardening and horticulture in general. His death
was a devastating blow, which 'deprived the gardening world
of an outstanding figure'. *Country Life* featured a homage to
'The Garden of a Great Gardener' in February 1942, written by
G.C. Taylor. The article celebrated 'the debt of gratitude' owed
to Lionel for his determination and devotion to 'his favourite
genus rhododendron', and it recalled his distinguished and
'enthusiastic labours', which had transformed 'what had been
largely an indeterminate quest for new kinds into a scientific

study of rhododendron hybridisation and culture'. The generous
sharing of his hybrids led Lord Aberconway to say, 'None of his
good plants did he ever wish to keep to himself, indeed the more
widely these were shared, the better he was pleased.'

In all things, Lionel showed an indomitable enthusiasm and
inexhaustible passion to reach for excellence. He drove so much
extraordinary change in so many diverse areas: plant hunting and
collecting, hybridisation, taxonomy, and horticultural charities
and organisations. His influence, skill and sheer energy were
transformative. Above all he was a woodland gardener and his
testament rests at Exbury. Taylor noted, 'On such a vast canvas
it is easy to make mistakes and produce a restless effect. But, by
a skilful disposition of the material, the division of the vast site
into sections each with its separate and distinct features, but all
connected to form a continuous whole, and planting with the bold
hand, demanded by the size of the place, such pitfalls have been
avoided. ... Despite its size it possesses a feeling of intimacy.'

Exbury's National Service · Years of turmoil and change

above
View of Gilbury bridge,
with different cultivars of
R. Naomi Group on right

left
The Rhododendron House,
destroyed by a bomb in the war

opposite, above
Exbury House with
R. 'Southamptonia' on right

opposite, right
Exbury House in the winter

Chapter Eight

Another contemporary, Viscount Templewood (1880–1959), compared Lionel's garden to the herbaceous borders of Philip Sassoon (1888–1939), a distant cousin as it happened: 'Both of them had unlimited money at their disposal, both also had the most discerning eyes for colour and effect, and both were past masters in that most necessary of the arts of life, the art of anticipation. ... Both could feel by instinct the effect of their designs.'

When Lionel died, some of his hybrids were yet to flower: his descendants would be first to witness them bloom. The perfect clear yellow of R. 'Crest', discussed in Chapter 5, was one. Another that only flowered after the war and was named after him (after a fashion) was the lovely peach-coloured R. 'Lionel's Triumph', a cross of R. *lacteum* and R. 'Naomi'. He was also honoured years later with a species named after him, R. *rothschildii*, a large-leaved rhododendron with creamy white flowers containing a crimson blotch.

Mariloo, enjoying the gardens in the post-war years

Ten years after his death, Mariloo summed up perfectly her immense pride in her husband's achievements and her deep sadness at his loss. 'I muse into the midst of bygone days, I cannot make up my mind whether to weep or smile, to live in the past or take courage and dive into the future.'

In fact, the part she played in keeping Exbury going after her husband's death was crucial. She emerged from his shadow not just as guardian of the flame but as a fine and knowledgeable judge of plants and planting in her own right. As her obituary in the *Year Book* put it, '[T]hough she claimed no horticultural expertise, she had an instinctive feeling for flowers of quality.' Exbury owes her a considerable debt of gratitude.

In May 1942, just four months after Lionel's death, Exbury was requisitioned by the Navy with immediate effect. This was part of a wider strategy at a critical time in the course of the war.

The English Channel was the only barrier to a full-scale invasion by Germany and the south coast had been massively fortified in anticipation of this threat. Large swathes of land across the south were used for training and the testing of new weapons and strategies.

The house was commissioned as a stone frigate (a sort of on-land naval establishment), HMS *Mastodon*, and thereafter acted as the Combined Operations base and training station for the Women's Royal Naval Service (the Wrens). Until the end of the war, in 1945, it would be closely involved in the Allied preparations for the Gold and Juno Sectors of D-Day, acting as a centre for training the landing craft crews used in the amphibious assaults on the Normandy coast.

Everyday life in Exbury changed irrevocably after the Navy's arrival. To enter the Beaulieu and Exbury areas of the New Forest involved getting a permit – 'a little pink piece of paper' – to travel through checkpoints and along the country roads to what was now a 'ship' and no longer a home. Areas of military importance were surrounded by five-foot-high barbed wire fences and the beaches at Lepe were off limits. Aeroplanes, tanks, searchlights, guns and all manner of equipment poured onto the roads. Three aerodromes were built in the New Forest, the nearest across the river at Beaulieu Heath. The forest provided excellent camouflage: a surprising amount of equipment and buildings could be hidden beneath the trees completely out of sight from above. On the Beaulieu River the landing craft and weapons accumulated around the riverbed to be worked on for D-Day preparations.

Many of the young soldiers who came to the area were in their early twenties, not used to country life at all, and found it to be rather quiet in the evening. However the pace of military life certainly kept them busy during the day. Nissen huts and tents were placed on the open lawns close to the house for the service personnel and Wrens who worked in the offices of the 'ship' and looked after the troops stationed there. Three large field kitchens were set up along the drive.

The gardens were put to use for growing food for the troops. The unheated peach case on the kitchen garden wall continued to grow fruit, and the glasshouses and Rhododendron House were used for tomato growing, despite bomb damage. The fields around the estate were ploughed for potatoes and vegetables; weekly deliveries to Covent Garden would be taken up by lorry to supply the city with fresh vegetables. As already mentioned, the orchid collection had largely been dispersed except for some of the cymbidiums, which were classified as a National Collection and kept going with a War Office grant for the coal to heat them – though even that collection was considerably reduced.

The whole south coast was highly fortified and HMS *Mastodon* played its part along with other D-Day bases; not far away was HMS *Vectis*, the Operations HQ of the British and Canadian forces at Cowes on the Isle of Wight, which was responsible for the assault on the Normandy beaches of Gold, Juno and Sword sectors. Anti-aircraft positions were placed on the coastline at Lepe, and Phoenix caissons – reinforced concrete breakwaters – that would protect the floating Mulberry harbours were run down the slipways on Lepe beach. Nearby at Beaulieu, Special Operations Executive (SOE) agents were trained to take on missions into enemy territory over the English Channel; likewise Inchmery House was used to train Free French, British commandos and Poles.

this page
Wartime letters from the gamekeeper, William Rattue, to Eddy; post-war view of Exbury House and the greenhouses

Preparations were at their height when George VI came to visit HMS *Mastodon* on 24 May 1944 and take the Royal salute. Captain Swinley, the organising officer at Exbury, told the Wrens to make themselves scarce, so a group of them hid in the ha-ha to catch a glimpse of the King. Once he had completed his military duties, he was due to be taken on a formal tour around the gardens: knowing his own way from his visits before the war, the King politely declined and disappeared alone for a few moments of quiet contemplation by the Top Pond.

opposite · Daffodil Meadow

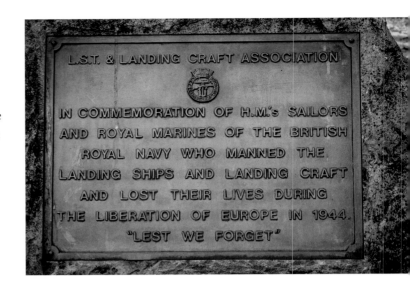

The mystery of the doomed German bomber

The story of a German Junkers Ju 188 which crash-landed on 18 April 1944 in fields in front of Exbury House has become an Exbury wartime legend, immortalised by Nevil Shute in his book *Requiem for a Wren* and explored by author John Stanley in *The Exbury Junkers: A World War II Mystery*.

Many service personnel stationed at the base, together with Exbury locals including Leo and Rosemary, who were staying at their mother's house, Marise Cottage, witnessed the early morning events. Narrowly missing the water tower, the damaged German bomber circled above Exbury House while bullets from two attacking Typhoons 'rebounded off the roofs of the Nissen Huts' and the doomed plane made its last attempt at landing.

Leading seaman, Reg 'Tug' Wilson was cycling back along a lane close by and on seeing the approaching German bomber he 'had to bike like hell to get out of the way' as the bomber crashed into the nearby pond in an area of the estate in front of the house known as 'the Park'. Its two engines 'came rolling though the hedge like two huge balls of twisted metal'.

Servicemen arriving at the scene hauled the seven-man crew as best they could out of the wreckage. Some were thrown clear on impact, but none were to survive, five killed on impact and two dying shortly after in the sickbay in the house. They were buried with full military honours at the nearby churchyard at Fawley; after the war they were reinterred at the German Military Cemetery on Cannock Chase and their names were read out in Exbury church at the annual Remembrance Sunday Service.

Why the Junker Ju 188 bomber was coming over the channel at such a fortified location and what the German seven-man crew were hoping to achieve is not absolutely certain but John Stanley

comes to convincing conclusions. While multifunctional, the plane had limited armament and was often used for reconnaissance or pathfinding. Was it on a reconnaissance mission? Was it deserting? It made no attempt to fight back or take evasive action and repeatedly fired off red distress flares.

It turns out it was moving from France to a forward base in Holland, in preparation for a pathfinding mission in support of a night raid on London, and held two ground support crew (recognisable by their uniforms) in addition to the air crew of five. It seems to have strayed off course from the European mainland, where there was poor visibility, to a clear-skied England and, despite electronic navigational equipment, realised its mistake too late; John Stanley concludes that it was most likely a compass malfunction compounded by the weather.

If the Ju 188 had returned to German-held airfields, 'Operation Fortitude' – the Allied plan to deceive the Germans into thinking the assault would mainly come across to Calais – might have been severely undermined. It seems certain that the two Typhoon aircraft that shot it down contributed directly to the secret delivery of the D-Day preparations along the Solent. However, those who witnessed the moment of impact and its aftermath saw at first hand the terrible price of war.

The woods at *Mastodon* were a temporary staging point for American troops following the first wave of the allied invasion of Normandy into France; many camped there before being shipped out to the front. Exbury was briefly renamed HMS *King Alfred* from January to June 1946 and then HMS *Hawke* in August 1946 and run as a training base. The house was finally decommissioned in 1955 after thirteen years of military occupation.

Having fought in the war himself, Eddy recognised the importance of honouring those who served at Exbury, and the Exbury Veterans Association has been active in holding reunions and exhibitions. The Arromanches plaque, unveiled by the Duke of Edinburgh in 1995, sits firmly in a block of Purbeck stone down by the side of the Beaulieu River to remind visitors today of the sacrifices made.

Eddy returned to Exbury in 1946. It was a very different place from the one he had known before the war and his own role in its development was to change too.

Exbury transformed

POST-WAR RESTORATION

CHAPTER 9

'[Lionel] would have approved of how his work
has been carried on with love and understanding
by his widow [and] by his elder son.'
Lord Aberconway

Born in the middle of one world war and a serving officer in a second, Lionel's elder son Edmund, (more commonly known as Eddy, or Mr Eddy to those at the bank and at Exbury) exemplified throughout his life a sense of duty – to his family, his community, his country and, of course, to Exbury Gardens.

Eddy returned to a home – and a village – much changed by the wartime occupation of Exbury and its aftermath. Rationing was in force. The requisitions by the armed forces in the New Forest and Solent area had changed the local landscape completely. The 'big house', still occupied by the Royal Navy, was no longer much of a source of employment and while essential tasks in the gardens still needed doing, increasingly people had to commute for much-needed work. The village could not resume the life it had enjoyed before, though it still very much retained a sense of community.

The family's situation had changed too: Lionel's widow, Mariloo, had moved to Marise Cottage, the decommissioned laundry in the village. Her move to a new home did not prevent Mariloo from continuing to play a central role at Exbury. A contrasting personality to her late husband, with a gentle and gracious demeanour (according to friends, her 'immense charm and warmth made people feel immediately at ease with her'), she was rarely seen at Exbury without a hat on her head and a pair of secateurs in her hand. She also remained sensitive to the British climate and tended to dress in many layers during all seasons of the year.

Mariloo took her role in village life seriously, through her participation in the Women's Institute and presence at village events. Above all she felt a deep responsibility for the gardens. She was determined that her husband's legacy and achievements at Exbury should be preserved for future generations. Not only that: she wanted to ensure her husband's contribution to the wider world of the rhododendron and horticulture generally would be remembered. While Eddy was away during the war, she had kept things going at Exbury, difficult though this was, for which he would always be grateful. Publicly she claimed,

'no horticultural expertise'; privately, however, she knew the gardens and the plant collections intimately, maintaining that she recognised individual rhododendrons better by studying their leaves rather than their blooms. She could regularly be seen walking around the gardens (later with her much-loved dog James), happy to share her horticultural knowledge or to recall stories of the past when she had trod those same paths with her late husband, whom she was to outlive by some 33 years.

There is no doubt that Eddy found his return from the war poignant. Many New Forest men did not return or else they came back to find the country much changed since their departure. Although he was secure at New Court and had a supportive family, Eddy too soon experienced the effects of post-war change. In the decade after the war many large country estates had to deal with escalating running costs and operate with a skeleton staff. Those estates that had been used for military purposes were often now in poor condition from years of institutional use and, like Exbury, were often not returned to the owners for over a decade or else were left to run down completely.

The war had another unfortunate legacy. People of all walks of life had suffered the loss of family members and the inheritance of estates needed to be weighed against post-war taxation and death duties. Some simply sold up, living abroad on the proceeds or moving to smaller homes within Britain. Many country houses were just abandoned or destroyed: in the 1950s over 400 country houses were demolished. Many others were transformed into schools, offices, apartments or hotels, signalling an end to their use as private homes.

Thus, in spite of Eddy's determination and optimism, Exbury still faced an uncertain future, not just as a family estate but as the home of one of the country's finest plant collections. For one thing, spare funds to sponsor any plant collectors out in the field simply did not exist. In any case, Eddy lacked the enthusiasm for it. It is also fair to say that, with civil war continuing between

154

clockwise from top left
At Inchmery: Mariloo, Jocelyne and
Naomi; Elizabeth with Nick, Charlotte,
Lionel and Kate; Elizabeth in the garden

previous pages · see page 197

Nationalist and Communist in China until 1949, followed almost immediately by Britain's involvement in the Korean War, the time was not exactly right for plant hunting in the Yunnan.

Rather, restoration was on Eddy's mind: how to rescue the gardens and the Exbury collection. He soon realised that if he was to take Exbury on and restore its fortunes he would need to live nearby. Inchmery had been occupied by his sister Rosemary and her first husband, Denis Gomer Berry (1911–1983), in the 1930s and then used during the war for training Free French, British commandos and Poles. Located right by the beach, it was a natural choice for Eddy and his new wife, Elizabeth (1923–1980) to bring up their growing family.

Despite the Admiralty being in residence at Exbury, a clause in the contract had allowed the gardens to be maintained by a limited staff. The team was led by the head gardener Francis Hanger (1901–1961) who had been at Exbury since 1927. However, in May 1945, exhausted by the war effort and keen for a new challenge, Hanger handed in his notice and moved to RHS Garden Wisley to take on the role of Curator. He had completed 18 years at Exbury and departed with the family's gratitude and best wishes for his future. Indeed he would go on to have an outstanding horticultural career at the RHS, a tribute to his experiences at Exbury. Plants that are named after him include *Camellia* x *williamsii* 'Francis Hanger', a white camellia with conspicuous deep yellow stamens, and R. 'Francis Hanger' a yellow-flowered rhododendron hybrid flushed with pale rose.

155

Many of Lionel's rhododendrons had been obscured by the neglect of wartime occupation but sometimes – as the years passed and parts of the gardens were cleared or as stock was re-evaluated – this led to outstanding discoveries. One in particular, the celebrated *Rhododendron yakushimanum*, would change the face of rhododendron breeding.

'Yak', as this species is known today by enthusiasts and horticulturalists alike, was recorded as the number one rhododendron of the twentieth century by members of the Rhododendron, Camellia and Magnolia Group for its centenary in 2016 (R. Loderi 'King George' was the top-ranked hybrid). Rightly so: its characteristics are distinct in so many ways. Its abundant and spectacular flowers are produced in late April–May, starting as rose-pink buds, then apple-blossom pink turning to white as the flower matures in tight round heads. The evergreen foliage is attractive throughout the year as the leaves appear tubular and featherlike and have woolly soft brown indumentum underneath. Yak's dwarf, compact, dense habit is as hardy in a sunny small garden as it is in a larger one. It is an ideal plant for gardens on lime-free soil.

R. yakushimanum was first discovered in the early 1900s on the small island of Yakushima, off the south coast of Japan. This is a subtropical mountainous island, a UNESCO World Heritage site since 1993, and long revered by the Japanese as one of the country's natural wonders. Lionel had been in correspondence with the Japanese nurseryman Koichiro Wada (1907–1981) of Yokohama Nursery; as ever, he was most interested in unusual and high quality plants and Wada clearly supplied both. In 1934 Wada sent a consignment of plants on the SS *Rawalpindi* via the Suez Canal and, along with various other treasures, two very small plants of Yak arrived at Exbury after their long trip; they cost 6/- each (another, at 10/-, was sent in 1938 but it is not known what happened to it). Lionel mentioned them in passing in his 'Notes on the Series of Rhododendrons' in the *Year Book of the Rhododendron Association* in 1937, oddly enough with the words, 'R. *yakusimanum*, with pale rose flowers, is not in cultivation'; perhaps he thought they had not survived, thus his ordering another the year after. The plants continued to grow slowly, seemingly unnoticed for many years.

On his departure to Wisley, Hanger took with him more than just the blessing of the family; one of the Yak seedlings went there too. He originally thought it was a layer from the plant he had seen arrive, though they were soon recognised as two distinct forms with interesting differences. In 1947 the Wisley plant was exhibited at the RHS Rhododendron Show and won a First Class Certificate. Three years later Eddy exhibited the Exbury plant at the Chelsea Flower Show with 'equally devastating effect'.

Yak soon became highly sought after by hybridists and has been the parent or ancestor of many a cultivar, though few if any can approach the original species for sheer beauty. It is now classified as a subspecies of *R. degronianum* and the form exhibited by Wisley, which won the FCC, has been given the cultivar name 'Koichiro Wada' in honour of this remarkable nurseryman. Over the years such varied growers as the Crown Estates, Windsor, Waterers, Hydon Nurseries, Millais, Harkwood Acres, Peter Cox, Ken Janeck, David Leach and Hans Hachmann in Germany have all focused on *R. yakushimanum* to produce excellent hybrids valued not only for their flowering quality but also for their foliage and hardiness.

Two of Lionel's legacies, *R. yakushimanum* and rhododendron trials, came together at a ten-year trial at the RHS, starting in 1996. Here many cultivars and hybrids were tested with the following objectives: to establish which, when grown well in full sun, remained compact, had good foliage and flowered well and consistently over a ten-year period; to determine any difference in habit, growth or performance between plants that had been grafted, micropropagated or grown from cuttings; and to investigate the effect if plants were not dead-headed. By the end of the trial, an astonishing 28 of those tested had received an AGM.

Lionel supposedly addressed the City Horticultural Society with the words, 'No garden, however small, should contain less than two acres of rough woodland' (he certainly wrote a similar remark). Yet the introduction of *R. yakushimanum* and its use in the creation of subsequent hybrids really did produce a new wave of rhododendrons for the small garden.

With Hanger gone, the search was launched for a new head gardener. Harold Comber had successfully collected for Lionel in the 1930s in Tasmania, South America and New Zealand. In 1946, however, shortly after his arrival and in spite of these excellent credentials, it soon became apparent the match would not work. One obvious problem was that Comber showed little interest in rhododendrons and more interest in other genera; his plant-hunting trips before the war had been to the Andes and Tasmania, neither places known for rhododendrons. Fine plantsman though he was, in terms of character too, he was perhaps not such a good fit.

His replacement was a better fit: Freddie Wynniatt (1910–1971), an experienced head gardener who had trained at Gosford House in Scotland, the seat of the Earls of Wemyss. Wynniatt had worked at Exbury before the war as a journeyman gardener from 1938 until he was called up for war duty. He was captured by the Germans and sent to work in an Austrian salt mine for much of the war. His return to the gardens after the war stimulated a devotion to them; he would go on to complete many years at Exbury.

The restoration of the gardens was a huge undertaking, beginning with clearing the brambles to reveal what had survived the inevitable years of neglect; everyone took part. A transformation had begun, one that would eventually be part of Exbury's rebirth as a popular public attraction.

It is true of course that, as a nation of garden lovers, the British have enjoyed a long tradition of garden visiting – stretching back to the tours of Viscount Cobham's (1675–1745) allegorical landscape gardens at Stowe, Buckinghamshire in the 1700s. In the Victorian era, the acclaimed Great Exhibition of 1851 brought the best of the Empire's horticultural influence together under one roof to great public excitement. Charlotte and later her son Leo, both avid gardeners, were keen to show visitors round the gardens and greenhouses at Gunnersbury. In Lionel's time, as we have seen, Exbury Gardens was occasionally opened to the public for charitable purposes. The RHS Chelsea Flower Show was reinstated in 1947 and while it continued to present flawless gardens, aimed increasingly to move away from its exclusive image and audience.

Like so many aspects of post-war life, public perceptions of gardens had changed. A post-war housing and population boom was under way and new housing estates were built around the country with smaller and smaller gardens. Meanwhile, the older generation's wartime vegetable production had been converted into the modern, youthful 'decorating' of the new garden with a fashionable colour scheme, and the media were full of glossy gardening articles and advertisements for day trips to stately homes and gardens to seek inspiration.

Lawrence Johnstone's Hidcote Manor Garden in Gloucestershire, gifted in 1948, was the first garden acquired by the National Trust. Nymans, the gardens of the Messels, was bequeathed to the National Trust in 1953. Times were changing for the country house and garden owners – and one major exhibition in particular underlined the renewed public interest in gardens and garden visiting.

The 1951 Festival of Britain at the South Bank, London, was heralded as 'a tonic to the nation ... to counter the continuing influences of the war on daily life' and mimicked the exhibition of 1851, offering Britain up as an industrial powerhouse ready to

Post Office and Stores, Exbury.

opposite
Exbury village shop;
bluebells and *Acer palmatum*

right
Hydrangea macrophylla
from Hydrangea Walk

take on the new global markets. As part of the Festival, 'a shop window for British horticulture' along the Thames was designed by the international landscape architect Russell Page (1906–1985). It proved a popular attraction with visitors. A grand vista mimicked the style of the great country houses of England, complete with towers, arcades, fountains, a miniature railway, a giant fern house and flower gardens, all sited in the northern part of Battersea Park and called the 'Pleasure Gardens'. Exbury supplied large specimen rhododendrons for the lawns. It was clear that the appetite for garden visiting had been reignited as a source of national pride; this new tourism market was an ideal opportunity for country houses and their gardens around the country.

For Eddy, there was a possibility that it would help to maintain Exbury Gardens and also offer some more employment to those living in the village or locally. He therefore decided that the family should share his father's legacy with a new audience. In 1955 Eddy opened Exbury Gardens to the public. The timing was certainly right. Increased personal income was allowing many more people from all walks of life to appreciate their newfound leisure time, and the wider affordability of cars meant that tourism and garden visiting were within the reach of many more Britons.

Peter Barber (1916–2006) had served with him in Italy and, as

his agent, he set in motion the transformation of Exbury Gardens. Advertising and marketing became part of the plan. The opening times appeared in the gardening press and in publications such as *Historic Houses, Castles and Gardens in Great Britain and Ireland*, issued by the British Travel and Holidays Association.

Xenia Field (1894–1998), the influential gardening correspondent of the day, and daughter of Tom Lowinsky (c.1858–1932), the owner of the Tittenhurst rhododendrons, embraced the story of the gardens, regularly featuring them in her *Daily Mirror* column. Even the Holborn Circus office windows of the paper were decorated with a spring display of Exbury rhododendrons in May 1963. In appreciation of her support, Eddy named one of his prize orchids, *Cymbidium* 'Xenia Field', after her.

The rhododendron had by now achieved the – no doubt rightful – position of one of the most fashionable plants of the day. The wider gardening press highlighted this with articles and practical advice on choosing the right rhododendron to make the perfect garden border. The public flooded into Exbury to see the now-famous spring display in the gardens. Cars were parked on the lawns and cuttings sold as mementos of a visit.

Exbury transformed · Post-war restoration

On open afternoons Eddy, 'jovial and avuncular', would often be present to welcome people. In the early years he would take an active role in brashing out the dead wood, and visitors would be surprised by a disembodied voice emerging from a thicket of rhododendrons with the words, 'Are you lost?'

As time went on, he preferred to drive his buggy around the paths of the gardens with his loppers, jumping out to introduce himself to unsuspecting visitors and leaping on an equally unprepared rhododendron that he felt needed tidying up. His enthusiasm was contagious. Visitors returned year after year to see the spectacular display of colour.

By 1979 the gardens were open every afternoon of the flowering season from April to June, with tickets costing 60 pence for adults and half that for children.

R. augustinii in Witcher's Wood

left
R. 'Leo'

opposite
R. 'Charlotte de Rothschild'

162 When the crowds had gone home, Eddy would talk to his plants. 'Well done! You really are a beautiful thing,' he would reassure one of his favourite hybrids (in the same bit of movie footage he follows this, to his children's amusement, by saying that if it did not flower, you should shake it and say 'Bad flower!')

With his own guests he would march through the woods regaling them with anecdotes, spoken in a booming voice just 'like a seasoned guide'. His father had seen the gardens as a broad canvas on which to arrange his vast collection of new plants; furthermore, as we have seen, he had an extraordinary eye for landscaping, and would sometimes time his tours to show plants to their best advantage, for example showing certain rhododendrons with the sun shining through them rather than on them. Eddy preferred to take his guests on a grand storytelling tour of the garden, showing off the best flowers depending on the season, pausing for a moment to tell an amusing tale about a plant, its name or origin. Lionel's legacy was to be celebrated, as Mariloo had always wanted, and the romance of Exbury endured.

Eddy had not just returned to the gardens and their management. He was also a senior figure in the bank where he was generous to the staff and much loved because of his interest in them and their lives. He was also extremely busy, spending a considerable amount of time away from Exbury, including frequent international travel.

Under the guidance of his uncle Anthony, Eddy initially oversaw the work of the Royal Mint Refinery, the very place where his father had propagated his orchids. In 1952 Winston Churchill introduced him to a new project in Canada, leading a consortium to fund the development of the vast hydroelectric potential of the Grand Falls on the Hamilton River in Labrador (later to be called the Churchill Falls Generating Station). Eddy would cross the Atlantic over 400 times during the 20 years the Churchill Falls project took to complete. At the time it was the largest civil engineering project ever undertaken in North America and still remains the second largest hydropower station in Canada.

Eddy also had dealings with Japan and loved going there. After the Second World War the bank started trading again with Japan and Eddy spent much time there on business, even learning to speak some rudimentary Japanese. This came in useful not just for work but for talking about plants and gardens; it eventually benefited Exbury as well.

Rhododendrons and azaleas had been imported to England from Japan since the mid-1800s and Leopold's Japanese garden at Gunnersbury and the Kurume azaleas that grow at

Exbury transformed · Post-war restoration

The 'Wiggly Tree', *Platanus orientalis*

Exbury epitomise the continuing influence of Japan on British gardening. Eddy enjoyed visiting the many iconic gardens in Japan, including a private view of the Imperial Palace Gardens. He later sent some Exbury azaleas to the Imperial Palace and was informed that the Emperor would visit them once a year at the height of their flowering. Links with Japan continue: his daughter Charlotte has visited Japan many times, where she sings in Japanese, specialising in 'Kakyoku' – Western style classical art songs of the nineteenth and twentieth centuries. Most recently, Exbury has been given a number of 'Noto Kirishima Tsutsuji', a rare and historic form of evergreen azalea, to be planted in Yard Wood, the first time they have been seen in the West.

EDDY'S GARDENERS

Eddy's gardeners: Douggie Betteridge (*front row, fourth from left*); Peter Barber, Eddy and Freddie Wynniatt (*middle row, third – fifth from left*)

During Eddy's tenure at Exbury the gardeners and their families were the beating heart of the gardens, devoting themselves to its restoration and upkeep. Freddie and Audrey Wynniatt, Douggie and Pearl Betteridge, Alf Gosney, Mike Molyneux, Ted and Laura Bartlett and Bill Hall all lived in the village, while their working lives revolved around Exbury House and Gardens.

Freddie Wynniatt was a rhododendron expert who instinctively knew the Exbury collections and how to care for them. Audrey, his wife, did the flowers for the house and helped out with special events, assisting with preparations of the exhibits for the shows.

Mechanisation had taken over the labour-intensive tasks like mowing, but digging, planting and clearing the overgrown gardens still had to be done by hand. The workforce used what remained of the glasshouses for Eddy's prize-winning cymbidiums, a few cattleyas and paphiopedilums, and the nerines. The fruit houses had survived the war and peaches, grapes and figs were much enjoyed by Eddy and his family.

During the flowering season, Freddie Wynniatt would ensure the gardens were kept in top condition. He also had a special spade put aside in case of a royal visit, an occurrence usually kept under wraps until the last moment.

As the representative of Exbury, Freddie regularly judged at horticultural shows and was a friend of the equally legendary Fred Nutbeam (1913–1997) who 'had two great qualities in a gardener, toughness and cheerfulness' and was head gardener at Buckingham Palace from 1954–1978. They frequently exchanged plants on behalf of their respective employers. A large group of Exbury hybrids and camellias were planted at Buckingham Palace in a bed behind the Tea House.

As the garden opening created a new source of income, so overgrown areas were restored and replanted to great success. There was no longer the unlimited stock from which to choose, as his father had, nor was Eddy so concerned with individual placing, delegating far more to his head gardeners. Furthermore – and certainly to judge from his choice of ties in later life – Eddy's taste was distinctly more kaleidoscopic. With Eddy's blessing, in 1964 Freddie set about creating the Azalea Bowl round the Middle Pond with vibrant colour; Lionel had already done something similar but had planted them in drifts. This was more dramatic: large numbers came in early May each year, to witness the reds, shocking pinks, purples and whites all massed together.

The Azalea Bowl

opposite · Eddy and Elizabeth; from left, Freddie and Audrey Wynniatt, Pearl and Douggie Betteridge   *above* · Audrey on the gate; Eddy at a flower show

The Azalea Bowl continues to be one of the most popular features of the gardens in spring. Freddie was awarded the A.J. Waley medal and the Associate of Honour by the RHS and the lovely orangey-striped R. 'Fred Wynniatt' was named after him by Eddy as a tribute to his outstanding contribution to Exbury.

Douggie Betteridge (1930–2018) joined Exbury having trained 'over the border' in a garden in Beaulieu. He and his wife Pearl became great friends of the Wynniatts. Douggie followed Freddie's daily routine: early start, lunch at 10 am and then back into the gardens until late. Often to be found working in the

depths of the gardens where, he said, 'even on the busiest days it is possible to be alone', he combined his plantsman's eye with a practical sense of the issues involved in running a 200-acre garden, open to the public. These included the watering system, the continual cutting back of the invasive R. *ponticum*, frost protection, deadheading, layering, pond maintenance and the all-important weeding.

Pearl handled the mail and was in charge of labelling the rhododendrons, sometimes keeping the labelling machine in the spare bedroom. During the peak spring season she took the ticket money at the entrance to the gardens, not

a small task when the queues of cars would back up past the Hill Top end of Summer Lane. The accountant Mr Thomas appeared every hour with a bag to decant the proceeds.

Throughout his life Eddy took great pride in attending the RHS shows. Exbury could always be relied upon to mount a good display and compete for prizes. At the crack of dawn, blooms were picked and Audrey Wynniatt carefully packed the heads of rhododendrons or camellias ready for the long journey to the RHS Halls in London. The display would be precisely set up, each delicate bloom unpacked and placed in a vase on the baize-covered exhibition

table. Minutes before the show started Eddy would arrive in a hurry from the bank, do a 10-degree turn of a bloom here, brush a single petal there and the Exbury display would be deemed ready for the show.

At the first peacetime RHS show in June 1945, 'magnificent' Exbury rhododendrons were proudly displayed. This was to be the norm, even in challenging circumstances. Despite the terrible 'Big Freeze' of 1962–1963, where some competitors did not make the Rhododendron Show, Exbury filled the RHS Hall in the prized spot under the clock with a gold-winning display.

above · Some of Douggie's team;
Douggie with R. 'Douggie Betteridge'

As Freddie had done before him, the weekend before the show Douggie would walk around the gardens with Eddy to discuss and recommend blooms for Exbury to exhibit. On one occasion Douggie suggested 'a beautiful unnamed pink rhododendron hybrid', but Eddy decided on another one. Luckily Douggie was prepared for anything. He recalled, 'When we came to take the blooms to Chelsea his chosen plant wasn't looking its best, so I quickly replaced it with the pink flower.' At the show, it won an Award of Merit and Mr Eddy was so delighted that he named it after him: R. 'Douggie Betteridge' (R. *fortunei* x R. Jalisco Group – appropriately it is a sibling of R. 'Fred Wynniatt', having the same parentage) still delights visitors today. A beautiful yellow rhododendron, R. 'Pearl Betteridge', was named after Douggie's wife after her too early death.

Exbury also won a number of awards for Eddy's favourite orchids – cymbidiums – at many RHS Orchid shows.

For camellias, Freddie won gold at the Spring Camellia Show in 1964, among many other awards during his tenure. At the Chelsea Flower Show Eddy achieved continued success to add to Exbury's record. For the 1951 show, the RHS installed what was supposedly the 'largest tent ever erected anywhere' and a headline reported 'Edmund de Rothschild's Exbury display showed its magnificent Kurume azaleas'. A 1956 gold-medal-winning exhibit of Exbury rhododendrons and azaleas was followed in 1959 with a triumphant woodland scene that also took gold. This success story continued. Years later, in 1992, Exbury won over 30 first prizes at the Rhododendron Show.

Douggie retired in 1995, only to return the next day, working on until 2013 when at the age of 81 he finally concentrated on his beloved vegetable plot, chitting his seed potatoes on the top of the wardrobe ready for planting the next season.

opposite · The Sundial Garden

Eddy's duties at the bank permitting, sharing the gardens with family, friends and experts continued. Eddy hosted lunches in a marquee erected on the lawn. Groups of guests were assigned a member of the family or staff who whisked them off into the gardens, come rain or shine, for a guided tour. The flavour or content of your tour very much depended on your guide: Eddy's elder son, Nicholas (Nick), followed his father in 'never letting the truth stand in the way of a good story', whereas his younger son, Lionel (the present writer), was and remains concerned with accuracy at all times. In addition to favourite anecdotes, plants or parts of the garden, those guiding also knew what would be flowering or which particular views to choose for maximum effect. Guests would leave, as Lionel's guests had all those years before, understanding what a unique place Exbury was.

The physical reshaping and repair of the gardens reaped rewards. However, the restoration of the rock garden, neglected in the years after Lionel's death, was certainly no project for the faint-hearted. In the late 1970s, under the guidance of Douglas Harris, then Managing Director, and led by head gardener Douggie Betteridge, all the team rolled up their sleeves as they restored this special part of the gardens to its former glory. They spent months clearing the enormous saplings that had sprung up between the rocks and, of course, the huge quantity of brambles.

Once the canopy was removed and they were released from their unwanted captivity, the surviving rhododendrons grew happily, but much replanting was needed. Initially this was done with rhododendrons already to hand, which happened to be predominantly purple, but over time the planting scheme has become more varied and, in addition to red, purple and yellow rhododendrons, it has grevillea, dwarf narcissi and a fringe of pieris along the western edge. In 2020, work started on further renovation of this great feature.

Change continued into the late twentieth century and beyond. The New Camellia Walk, running parallel to part of the old one, was created in 1996 and was the inspiration of Douggie's successor, Paul Martin; it displayed many American hybrids including the deep red C. 'Bob Hope' and the exquisite white C. 'Nuccio's Jewel', and New Zealand hybrids like C. 'Jury's Yellow'. It was also planted up with a selection of magnolias, both M. x *soulangeana* hybrids and M. *stellata* cultivars, and these, coming between the camellias and the canopy of crown-lifted *Thuja plicata*, *Sequoiadendron giganteum* and Monterey pines, lighten the overall effect. Lionel, who clearly liked to layer his planting, would have approved.

In 2006 a collection of 300 camellias was donated by the horticulturalist and third-generation camellia expert Jennifer Trehane and planted in the Gilbury Lane Garden that runs just near the playground and entrance; these and additional plants form a fine new feature. In 2014 Exbury Gardens was awarded the prestigious title of 'Camellia Garden of Excellence' by the International Camellia Society.

The Sundial Garden always had a wonderful intimacy, with a style reminiscent of garden designer and plantsman Lawrence Johnston's (1871–1958) garden 'rooms' at the influential Hidcote Manor Garden. It is one of the few formal areas of the gardens, surrounded by yew hedge. The sundial topped with a griffin was originally at Inchmery but after that house was sold in 1987 and the family moved back to Exbury House, it was moved to this garden – hence the name.

An old photograph shows it planted out with a bedding scheme of tulips; then, after the war, it had a rather unsuccessful arrangement of rose beds. Nick eventually redesigned the rose garden with a mixture of standard roses and alliums in mirror beds with lavender edging, a large pair of tree ferns, *Dicksonia antarctica*, and a yellow laburnum on the arch at the river end gate. In 2004 this was changed, retaining the mirror scheme but replacing the roses and alliums with a mixture of bright herbaceous and exotic plants, including orange flowered cannas and purple flowered tibouchina, all selected to look their best in late summer.

At one end of the Sundial Garden there is a large pergola made of Portland stone covered by an enormous *Wisteria floribunda* 'Macrobotrys'. After the all too premature death of Eddy's beloved and beautiful wife Elizabeth, this little garden was dedicated to her. A curved bench stands in her memory inside the pergola.

In the early days, however, the reshaping of the gardens posed new problems. When the gardens first opened in the 1950s, the visiting public parked their cars on the lawns near the house and a small plant centre and restaurant facilities were created there. The sheer number of people led to long queues and the sheer number of cars – and above all the effect of their tyres on the lawns – led to increased wear and tear on the fabric of the garden.

A solution was found. A whole new parking area was created in the old estate yard over the bridge, the smithy was converted into a restaurant, the plant centre relocated and a proper entrance office constructed: things were becoming professional. In place of the old plant sales area, the vibrant Herbaceous Borders were laid out beside the house; these have since been expanded. Filled

172

above · R.'Drury Lane'

with contemporary textural planting, they continue to be a greatly admired part of the gardens and give a dramatic show of colour in the summer months; they are ably looked after by Exbury's invaluable team of volunteers.

The upkeep of the gardens has not just been supported by paying visitors, however. In the post-war period the wholesale production of trees and shrubs in the Top Nursery for sale around Britain and the world took off. The main competitors were some of the big names in commercial plant production and sale – Hillier, Sunningdale, Notcutts and Slocock. All survived the war and these nurserymen took the lead over the now diminished amateurs, producing and distributing hardy trees and shrubs through the newly established garden centres and mail order catalogues.

Technology changed too: mist propagation was introduced in the 1950s and plastic pots became widespread in the 1960s; later still, automatic watering systems in polythene tunnels further reduced costs. Plant catalogues grew ever more comprehensive and, with better colour photography, enticing.

Exbury, it seems, was ready for the challenge. The domestic market wanted plants that would give them a blaze of colour and Exbury's answer was to scale up and use Exbury as a resource. The ebullient Peter Barber claimed on a tour of America, '[W]e are probably the largest growers of rhododendrons, azaleas and allied plants in the country, something like a quarter of a million rhododendrons of all types ... one hundred thousand camellias, with evergreen and deciduous azaleas in like numbers.' As for hybridisation, Eddy knew that the scale of amateur breeding since the First World War could never happen again. Nevertheless the Exbury hybridisation programme continued on a smaller scale. Cuttings and layering of the Exbury hybrids were undertaken and new colours were developed; for sale, they concentrated on hybrids that would prove hardy and have the largest possible flowers.

The new Exbury azalea strains were brightly coloured and with broad petals, some with brilliant blotches, some scented, often flowering for over a month – and they were loved by the American market. In fact large quantities were exported to nurseries around the world, including the Girard and Arneson nurseries in America. American plant suppliers Wade Robbins and John Henny and importer Jock Brydon hybridised them further, following the mantra 'use the best from each generation to get better'. The flowers of the Knap Hill strain of Exbury hybrids could reach four inches in diameter and came in impressive shades of yellow, orange and red as well as white and pink.

Hybrids have provided a number of crowd-pleasing plants over the years. In 1959–1960, Freddie Wynniatt managed the acquisition of a new range of deciduous azaleas which the nurseryman and expert hybridist George Hyde (1916–1980) had bred using Exbury azaleas at Ferndown, Dorset. Eddy went to view the azaleas *en masse* on a hastily arranged tour of the nursery. Recognising their beauty and quality, he immediately made an offer for the collection, which he then named the 'Solent' range. Many of these are planted down Lover's Lane and generally have a more rounded head than the Exbury azaleas. Notable ones include R.'Citroen', yellow with some orange flushing, R.'Beaulieu Manor', red flushed orange, and perhaps one of the best of all, R.'Drury Lane', orange-yellow with tips of pink. Of course, when Exbury Gardens opened to the public R.'Crest' (FCC 1953) was the pure yellow plant that everyone wanted to see. Eddy believed that 'Crest' was 'without a doubt my father's best yellow hybrid',

adding that it 'draws the crowds around it like a magnet'.

Naturally Eddy named more of his father's hybrids. For his elder daughter Kate, he chose one with large white trusses with a dark red throat, R.'Our Kate' (sadly prone to frost damage); for his younger daughter, Charlotte he chose a spectacular and stately pink rhododendron, R.'Charlotte de Rothschild'. R.'Nicholas', a chance R. *ponticum* hybrid, was a lucky find: naming it after his elder son, Eddy liked to say, 'I know who the female parent is, but the identity of the male parent is known only to the bees!' While he did not undertake hybridising on anything like the scale of his father, nevertheless the material proved irresistible to build upon. He loved the bold flowers of R.'Kilimanjaro', one of the best large red hybrids made by his father, and used this to produce R.'Edmund de Rothschild' – like its namesake, splendid and sturdy; it won an FCC in 1993. He used R.'Lionel's Triumph' to create R.'Elizabeth de Rothschild',

Eddy always saw the positive, particularly if Exbury could help other gardens. In January 1968 a hurricane hit Scotland with such force that many of the great Scottish rhododendron gardens that Lionel had known so well were devastated. Eddy promised that 'Exbury ... of course [is] ready to send some plants up for the great rebuilding that hopefully must come.'

Exbury itself was badly affected by the drought of 1976, which saw the water table drop dramatically, killing numerous plants and highlighting the need for a reservoir. The hurricane of 1987 and the great storm of 1990 caused terrible damage: the saddest casualties of all were a number of the huge ancient cedars from the Mitford era that lined the glade. Eddy stayed up all night long listening to the howling storm wreaking havoc, but he was not discouraged. In fact he saw this as an opportunity for renewal in the garden: the stripping away of the dense canopy revealed previously hidden plants, allowing new vistas and new plantings to be created and a fresh beauty to be brought to the gardens.

In 1989, accompanied by his second wife Anne (née Kitching) (1921–2012), Eddy spoke at the American Rhododendron Convention on Vancouver Island, Canada, something his younger son Lionel did again in 2015. His audience were dismayed to hear of the first storm and when, shortly after his return, the second one hit, they arranged for a substantial shipment of American hybrids to be sent. These were planted in Yard Wood and, with the addition of azaleas and yellow laburnum, form the American Garden.

175

an attractive pale yellow-green with maroon spotting in the throat. New material also became available, for example the deep yellow R. 'Hotei', a hybrid originally from the United States, which he used to make one of the best of Exbury's more recent hybrids, the compact-growing R. 'Jessica de Rothschild', light greenish yellow and stronger yellow at the centre, with yellowish pink tips.

One area that neither science nor skill could do much about was the weather. Long before Eddy took over, the weather loomed large in Lionel's gardening correspondence. He was all too aware of the rain shadow cast by the Isle of Wight, pushing the clouds up over the gardens only to open over Hill Top and beyond. He wrote continually of the threat of frost in the gardens (although sometimes an early one would result in the most glorious blooms in the spring). The 'blizzard of the decade' of January 1940 was the worst he experienced.

Historically, American gardens appeared in Victorian England in the 1830s to house the conifers and evergreens from the collectors of North America and Canada and it is thus appropriate that towering above the American Garden is the tallest evergreen tree in the Exbury collection, *Abies grandis*, from the Pacific Northwest, reaching around 37 metres in height.

Deciduous azaleas and laburnum in the American Garden

Chapter Nine

TREE-PLANTING CEREMONIES

Eddy with the Queen Mother (*left*) and with the Queen (*above*)

opposite · R. elliottii at the bottom of Witcher's Wood

A little to the north of the American Garden is the oldest tree, called the Domesday Yew. Trees are not mentioned in the Domesday Book and, at between 300–400 years old, this one is nothing like as old as the Domesday Book of 1086. Nonetheless it is venerable (and hollow) and perhaps its association with regeneration and transformation is appropriate for this part of the garden.

Trees have other strong associations for the gardens. Exbury has continued to host many royal visits and of course no royal visit would be complete without a tree planting ceremony. The Queen, the Queen Mother, Princess Margaret, Prince Charles and Prince Michael of Kent have all picked up the spade for posterity and added to the diverse collection of specimen trees that flourishes in the gardens.

On a very wet day in 2004 the Queen planted a new young yew, *Taxus baccata*, a little way down from the Domesday Yew. Other Royal families have also planted trees, including the King of Sweden in the garden's inaugural year of 1955 and the Queen of Bhutan in 1967. Eddy's 21st birthday and his sister Rosemary's 90th were another good excuse to find new specimen trees to adorn the garden.

Eddy had overseen the restoration and replanting of much of the gardens and, though it is important to stress that the structure remained very much as his father had laid it out, he introduced new features. The planting of the Solent range of deciduous azaleas down Lover's Lane has already been mentioned. In addition to the American Garden, two other developments took place in Yard Wood. On the way to the Rock Garden, a low-lying damp area was turned into a Bog Garden. On a path down to Jubilee Pond, Eddy planted a lovely collection of lacecap *Hydrangea macrophylla*, the Teller hybrids developed in Switzerland. These were raised at the Federal Research Institute for Horticulture at Wädenswil, Switzerland and a donation of 26 were given to him 1992. They are mostly named with different bird names in German and 'Teller' means 'saucer' in German,

after their characteristic shape. Finally, in complete contrast to the main garden, Eddy opened up River Walk. As its name suggests, River Walk follows the edge of the Beaulieu River to View Point, the furthest point in the Winter Garden; another section of River Walk has now been added, running from the very bottom of Daffodil Meadow to the inlet of the creek below Bottom Pond. These walks wind their way through pedunculate oaks on the river margin and give walkers a chance to see and hear some of the marsh birds.

The post-war story of the Rothschilds and Exbury does not entirely belong to Eddy and his team, however. His brother Leo, numerous skilled gardeners and designers and the next generation have all played a part in helping to build modern-day Exbury, whose evolution we shall address in the next chapter.

this page · Autumn leaves fallen in the water   *following pages* · *see page 197*

A place to cherish

EXBURY TODAY AND BEYOND

CHAPTER 10

As Eddy advanced in years, re-evaluation of the gardens and their future was needed; leading these changes was his younger brother Leo. He too had become a partner at the bank and, like his great-uncle Alfred before him, sat as a director on the Court of the Bank of England.

But, like his father and brother, he too had other interests – and, while gardening occupied some of his time, music was, arguably, central to his whole life. Leo recalled of his mother, '[S]he wanted me to learn the violin, but I made such a terrible noise that when I asked to switch to piano she welcomed the idea with open arms.' Although he always said of himself that he was a frightful piano player, his friends knew otherwise. He supported many leading musical charities and organisations including

fundraising for the creation of the Britten Theatre at the Royal College of Music. Another interest was the Bach Choir, in which he sang for over 50 years, and a beautiful rhododendron, purplish pink going more yellow to the centre, has been named R.'Bach Choir'. In 1985 he was appointed CBE for services to music and musical charities.

However, he was also highly influential in the evolution of Exbury. In fact his innate qualities of clarity and caution meant he saw the need to safeguard the future of the gardens. In order to ensure the gardens were preserved for the public benefit and to advance horticultural knowledge through them, at the end of the 1980s Leo created and generously endowed a new charitable trust, The Exbury Gardens Trust, to support the gardens into the future. Both this and the charitable trust which owns the gardens themselves share nearly identical objects, principally the 'maintenance, improvement, development and preservation for the public benefit of Exbury Gardens in Hampshire'.

He was also among the first to realise the importance of modern approaches to record-keeping. A notable ground-breaking initiative approved by Leo was the cataloguing of the plant collections at Exbury. This was a very ambitious proposal; an 'inventory' of the gardens had never been undertaken. Some rhododendrons are long-lived – certainly many trees are – and while the stud books, Lionel's card index files and a few remaining labels gave clues as to what had been planted, and where, capturing this information in a database for future use was a relatively novel concept at the time, needing new methodology.

this page and right
Leo at his desk and the view from the engine;
the steam train among the cherry blossom

The task was entrusted to Michael and Beverley Lear, a husband-and-wife team, working in the landscape design, development planning, and heritage spheres. It was decided to concentrate on rhododendrons, deciduous azaleas, camellias and specimen trees and shrubs but to exclude evergreen azaleas for the time being. The project team drew up a plan of 340 plots within the 200-acre site to enable them to work systematically. Over an eleven-year period, from 1990 to 2000, they recorded key data using Psion organisers – barely remembered now but the latest technology at the time.

A short flowering season demands intense focus on a project such as this. From early morning to late evening the pace of identification and labelling was exhausting. A host of books, new and old, and the RHS Colour Chart formed the basis of the identification, with rulers on hand for recording dimensions. Every once in a while a 'red pen day' took place to sort out the trickier identifications. Groups of rhododendrons were shown to Douggie Betteridge who then adjudicated, drawing on the characteristics of the leaf, flower shape and colour, bark, scent, form and size.

The team felt they were treading in Lionel's footsteps, following the thought patterns of his planting, peeling back the historic layers of the gardens and documenting the way he combined colour, texture and form to create his gardens. The cataloguing revealed how Exbury is unique and why Lionel's creation truly is exceptional.

A grand total of 17,000 woody plants were recorded, the largest survey of its time ever undertaken and a benchmark for heritage gardens around the world. The database has been continued and updated and is now on the widely-used IrisBG (Botanical Garden Collection Management) software; it provides a wealth of information that has supported Exbury Gardens in the preservation and expansion of the collection. The Exbury database now shows 6,000 different taxa and lists some 24,000 plants or groups of plants, of which 13,000 accessions are rhododendrons. Lionel, with his detailed card indexes, would have been proud. It is a huge credit to Leo and the current generations of the family that they continue to endorse the importance of recording plant data for posterity.

clockwise from top left
Leo in his railway uniform;
detailing at the station; Eddy

'Ever since I can remember I've loved steam engines. I must have been born with a kind of virus – a virus that affects many other people who are normally perfectly sane.'

Music was not the only passion of Leo's life. Leo, who dreamt of the 'whiff of coal, steam, hot oil' for over 60 years, was a self-confessed 'railway nut'. This obsession came together with a brand-new garden to form another of Leo's gifts to Exbury: the Exbury Gardens Steam Railway.

For his 70th birthday he hired a steam railway to bring his guests down from London and promised them that in five years time, they would ride on his own. A project team that had been assembled to manage the planning, landscaping and installation of a railway set to work in the gardens in early 2000. Leo's childhood friend, the award-winning architect

Sir James Dunbar-Nasmith (b.1927), was appointed as architect and eventually over 200 people were involved in the project – particularly challenging given the unusually wet winter that year.

The track chosen was 12¼-inch gauge and a whole new garden was created for it in the area of an old quarry: this was named the Summer Lane Garden. Filled with herbaceous plants, it featured a little red iron bridge and a curved tunnel; each end of the tunnel was different and the splendid castellated end was based on a famous Gothic folly, the Clayton Tunnel North Portal in West Sussex. The track was then routed through existing parts

Leo tightened the last coach screw on the track on 3 August 2001; steam engine trials were then carried out to ensure everything ran smoothly. True to his promise, the actual launch was 12 May 2002, his 75th birthday – Leo's present to himself and to the gardens.

The railway was a great hit with the public: both the Ghost Train at Halloween and the Santa Special at Christmas have proved especially popular. The Queen has visited twice, in 2004 and 2008, and each time Her Majesty rode on the footplate with Leo driving, both clearly enjoying themselves tremendously. Leo's hope, that it would give years of pleasure to all generations, has been realised.

In 2017 the line was extended from one and a quarter miles to one and a half, and the new 'Dragonfly Halt' was added beside a pond now renamed Dragonfly Pond, the aim being to create a wildlife habitat to attract these wonderful and extraordinary insects. The Rothschild passion for entomology has run through many members of the family, including Walter Rothschild of Tring Park, the great naturalist, and his niece, Miriam Rothschild (1908–2005). Ruary Mackenzie

Dodds and his wife Kari de Koenigswarter (Miriam's niece), both great dragonfly experts, have advised on the project, which adds a new educational and environmental dimension to Exbury's summer attractions.

When Leo died in 2012, he asked that his very considerable collection of 'railwayana' – pictures, models, memorabilia – be sold at auction specifically to benefit his railway. The proceeds were used to reroute the line and create the new halt, as described. Leo, who had done so much to help Exbury become the popular attraction it is today, did not live to see recent developments, although he was able to enjoy the early years of the railway, frequently spending all day driving the engine himself.

In 2005, 75 years after his father, Eddy was awarded the

VMH at the RHS Hampton Court Flower Show for his whole-hearted enthusiasm for the rhododendron genus and his tireless work continuing the family tradition at Exbury Gardens: it was a just recognition for embracing his father's horticultural legacy with such devotion. He had served on the RHS Council in the 1960s – when rhododendrons were at something of a fashionable peak – and supported the work of the RHS ever since. Eddy died at Exbury on 17 January 2009, shortly after his 93rd birthday. His widow would follow him in November 2012. His obituary in the *The Daily Telegraph* said, 'he was a man of irrepressible optimism and good nature and saw only the best in others. He was trusting and generous to a fault'.

185

of the garden, passing along the edge of the Rock Garden, round past the Domesday Yew and stopping at a halt in the American Garden before returning home.

A station modelled on Aviemore in Scotland was built, along with an engine shed, turning circle and siding. The metal frame of the station was clad in timber fretwork and decorated with special iron brackets featuring the Rothschild family's five arrows device, forged by the 200-year-old Ballantine Bo'ness Iron Company of Bo'ness in Scotland.

The engines and carriages were all named after female members of the Rothschild family – the engines are called 'Rosemary', 'Naomi' and 'Mariloo' – and were all built by Trevor Stirland of the Exmoor Steam Railway, North Devon, an expert narrow-gauge steam railway engineer. Smiling broadly, Leo was heard to say that they 'looked and sounded absolutely splendid'.

For his 90th birthday Eddy was given a bench, deliberately located round an oak tree near his favourite R. Fortune Group rhododendrons and inscribed with the words, 'It was his good fortune to inherit these gardens. It was their good fortune to inherit him.'

opposite · Nerines, see page 196

The Exbury Gardens Trust today is dedicated to preserving the gardens and plant collections in perpetuity for the enjoyment of the public, thanks to the initiatives put in place by Eddy and Leo. As a heritage collection, the gardens are a unique resource for the advancement of horticultural science, knowledge and botanical learning. The Exbury name continues to be held in high regard for the quality of hybrids produced there; furthermore, there is an ongoing programme of propagating hybrids and species within the collection through a variety of different techniques, including micropropagation and more conventional means such as grafting, layering and taking cuttings. Exbury continues to foster good relationships with other horticultural organisations, exchanging plant material and knowledge with them.

At Exbury Gardens there is commitment to the encouragement of wildlife and a belief in a light touch so that natural environments can thrive. A bequest from Leo's cousin and fellow trustee, Renée Robeson (1927–2015) has and will be used to plant the native English trees, above all oaks, so vital for the future canopy. The gardens are a haven for different species of wildlife that live along the margins of the river, in the meadows, in the mature oak trees scattered throughout the woodlands and in the many and varied ponds. From spring to summer the bluebells, primroses, daffodils and wildflowers – including the green-winged orchid – entice butterflies, bumblebees and many other insects. From midsummer to autumn the herbaceous borders become the focus of a buzzing frenzy, while damselflies and dragonflies hover around the ponds.

Over 1,000 species of fungi thrive in the gardens, which also provide a habitat for a host of invertebrates and 50–60 bird species such as the song thrush, the goldcrest and firecrest, spotted woodpeckers and goshawks. A family of ravens can be heard 'cronking' in the early evening. On the river margin near the Arromanches plaque, teal, curlew, lapwing and even, occasionally, an otter can be spotted. Badgers, foxes and deer are residents of the undergrowth, while bats and owls bring the night skies alive.

Visitors can enjoy the changing of the seasons every day of the week from mid-March to early November, after which the gardens close to the public for an annual programme of maintenance and care.

Exbury's collection of nerines ('Jewel Lilies' or 'Guernsey Lilies') is unrivalled. Curated by Lionel's grandson Nick, this collection has its own colourful history. It now consists of about 1,000 cultivars of one species, *Nerine sarniensis*, the largest known in the United Kingdom. This tender glasshouse flower is dormant in the summer, producing an umbel of funnel-shaped flowers in

A place to cherish · Exbury today and beyond

the autumn, followed soon after by strappy leaves. Nerine petals emerge in a spectrum of colours from their original oranges through new whites, pinks, reds, scarlets, coppers, purples and mauves. In bright light, whether natural or artificial, the facets on the petals appear to sparkle silver or gold.

They grow prolifically on the slopes of Table Mountain overlooking Cape Town, South Africa, and were first recorded in 1635. Linnaeus called them *Amaryllis sarniensis* in 1753 and the nerine genus was later established by Rev. William Herbert (1778–1847), who wrote a monograph on it in 1820. At Exbury, following in the footsteps of H.J. Elwes of Colesbourne Park, Lionel took on the mantle of breeding nerines in the 1920s–1930s, coming up with a number of classic blooms.

While bulbs may flower in the first season of planting (depending on the age and size of the bulb) plants grown from fresh seed may take between five and nine years to flower: the novice grower has no reason to be scared but the novice breeder has a long wait ahead of him. Lionel had plenty of experience in waiting for plants to flower, so they were in safe hands at Exbury, thriving in a cool greenhouse. After the war the collection was revived by Eddy but in 1972 he sold most of the nerines to Blackmore and Langdon's, growers of begonias and delphiniums. He did keep a handful back for a very special purpose: the Queen Mother was Patron of the Garden Society and every year after its autumn dinner Eddy would present her with a bouquet of nerines.

Two years later, Blackmore and Langdon's sold off the collection piecemeal. The best bulbs were acquired by the venerable plantsman, Sir Peter Smithers (1913–2006), a British diplomat and wartime colleague of Ian Fleming (1908–1964), creator of James Bond. As a young man, he lived at Itchen Stoke House, and in his twenties knew Lionel's daughter, Naomi. Later he was MP for Winchester and then Secretary-General of the Council of Europe (1964–1969). His exceptional garden at Vico Morcote overlooking Lake Lugano, Switzerland, was filled with plants that he loved including magnolias, tree peonies, lilies, wisteria and, in greenhouses, clivias, amaryllis, hibiscus and cacti. A beautifully scented daphne bears his name, *Daphne bholua* 'Peter Smithers'. He was remarkably proficient at everything he turned his hand to and his highly entertaining autobiography, *Adventures of a Gardener* (1995), is filled with fabulous photographs he took with a large-format field camera. His gardening philosophy was that a garden 'should be a source of pleasure to the owner and his friends, not a burden and an anxiety'; his own was planted so that

its maintenance decreased as it matured and he aged.

He had already experimented with nerines but now he undertook a careful and selective programme after Lionel's heart – but he did not wish to rely on his own taste alone. Every year, therefore, he would stage a 'Beauty Contest' where his guests would vote and were told to 'forget about any consideration except beauty as they see it'. The winning nerine was toasted with a glass of champagne.

Later still, as old age started to catch up on him, he looked for a suitable home for the collection. In 1995 he sold it to Exbury, and thus it returned home, vastly improved, this time to a large modern glasshouse. As bulbs divide and multiply over time, what started as a modest collection has expanded dramatically to remarkable proportions. Notable cultivars include: N. 'Exbury Eddy', a vibrant red; N. 'Amschel', a fine dark purple with a red stripe; N. 'Marie-Louise Agius', pale pink; N. 'Kalahari Dawn', mauve with pink tips and N. 'Heart's Delight', orange with a white throat. They are looked after by Theo Herselman, originally from Zimbabwe. Every October, Theo mounts a spectacular and artistic display of nerines in the Five Arrows Gallery and every March he mounts another display, this time of lachenalias (again a South African bulb), orchids and tender rhododendrons; these displays book-end the opening season.

opposite · N. 'Copperhead'   *above* · from left, Nick, David Millais, Tom Clarke, Kate, Marcus, Lionel, Charlotte, Marie-Louise

Kate is an expert on Old Master Drawings and serves as a trustee of the Wallace Collection. She particularly cherishes the aesthetic beauty of her grandfather's legacy at Exbury. Her husband, Marcus Agius, a keen gardener, has served as chairman of the trustees of the Royal Botanic Gardens, Kew and is now chairman of Exbury Gardens Limited.

Nick has made two films about the gardens, *The Glory of the Garden* (1982) and *Heaven with the Gates Open* (2001). He curates the nerine collection and has an interest in South African bulbs generally. He enjoys taking photographs which he then digitally manipulates in the style of a painting.

Charlotte is an internationally renowned lyric soprano who sings in over 20 languages, most notably Japanese, performing regularly all over the world. She creates themed programmes of songs, among which are her 'Family Connections' programme, comprising music by friends, teachers or relatives of the Rothschilds and, appropriately, her 'Flower Songs of the Seasons'.

Lionel is closely involved with running the gardens through chairing The Exbury Gardens Trust. He co-authored *The Rothschild Gardens* (1996) with his cousin Miriam and has written various articles on rhododendrons and on Exbury. He is also a trustee of The Rothschild Archive London and sits on the Garden Council at Borde Hill Garden.

190   The next generation is already making its mark as custodians
        of Exbury. Marie-Louise Agius, daughter of Kate and Marcus, is
        a Chelsea Flower Show Gold Medal winning garden designer,
        specialising in landscaping projects. She is the designer of the
        Centenary Garden at Exbury. This stylish garden, occupying what
        was once a tennis court surrounded by yew hedging, reflects
        the enduring strength of Exbury Gardens into the twenty-
        first century. The contemporary design makes the most of the
        summer season, featuring mirrored herbaceous borders, clipped
        Myrtus communis balls, climbing roses, golden fastigiate ginkgos,
        and cloud-pruned azaleas behind a curved floating bench. The
        overall design of the garden references the formal layout and
        mirror planting of the adjoining Sundial Garden. The five arrows
        take central place in a sunken paved circle. Exbury Gardens were
        honoured by HRH The Prince of Wales who came formally to
        open the Centenary Garden in July 2019.

above and right
Prince Charles and Marie-Louise Agius;
the Centenary Garden

Fortune has continued to favour Exbury with some highly skilled and professional head gardeners and advisers. Nurseryman and horticulturalist Douglas Harris did much to improve the gardens during his tenure as Managing Director in the 1970s, most notably the restoration of the Rock Garden, and he recently supplied some of his beautiful hamamelis. Since the 1980s the management has been under the direction of Smiths Gore (now Savills) and their partner Adrian Neal.

The work of the head gardener remains paramount. After Freddie Wynniatt and Douggie Betteridge came Paul Martin, who had worked at Mount Stuart on the Isle of Bute in Scotland; he designed the New Camellia Walk, mentioned earlier. Then came Rachel Foster who was originally at Trebah in Cornwall. Her tireless work in beautifying the gardens is much in evidence today.

After Rachel the post was filled by John Anderson, who had been at Mount Usher in Ireland and Inverewe in Scotland. With his truly encyclopaedic knowledge of trees John realised that, while many specimens had been lost with the destruction of the arboretum and while many remained in the gardens themselves, there was scope for further accessions. John added extensively to the collection and wrote the pocket-sized *A Guide to the Trees of Exbury* (2012), which gives an overview of many of the finest and rarest trees and shrubs. Exbury gained National Plant Collection status for its nyssas and oxydendrum during his tenure and these plants boost the autumn colour in Yard Wood. Also in Yard Wood, he planted a swathe of different varieties of *Hydrangea paniculata* along a stretch of Azalea Drive – thus extending the season of visual impact in this area – and, honouring Lionel's fondness for cotoneasters, planted a selection of them opposite the hydrangeas. In 2016 John accepted the prestigious role of Keeper of the Gardens at Windsor Great Park and was awarded a VMH in 2020. It is a credit to Exbury that its head gardeners go on to such high-profile posts and honours.

John has been succeeded by Thomas Clark: Tom had worked mainly at Trelissick and more briefly at Glendurgan and Tregothnan, all outstanding woodland gardens in Cornwall, thus gaining a perfect grounding in acid-loving plants. John had known Tom from plant-hunting expeditions they had made together, something Exbury is keen to support in the future. The various gardens listed above, both private and National Trust, in which Exbury's head gardeners had worked before coming to Exbury, act as testament to the woodland garden tradition in the British Isles and to the calibre of the gardeners it produces.

Miscanthus sinensis 'Yakushima Dwarf' in the Centenary Garden

Tom will ensure Exbury Gardens thrives, with the continued support of The Exbury Gardens Trust and the Rothschild family, into its second century. The current leadership of the team at Exbury Gardens, following in the footsteps of some exceptional head gardeners, falls on Tom's calm and capable shoulders: during the Covid lockdown of spring 2020, with everybody else on furlough he did all the gardening himself – and rather enjoyed doing so. He has instigated a programme of rejuvenation of certain areas, one of which is the Iris Garden, which has been opened up, enlarged and replanted. He is also keen to employ modern technology and in the lawn opposite the Iris Garden two great swathes totalling 150,000 bulbs – in a mix of the family colours of blue and yellow – were planted in honour of the centenary in a mere three hours using a special machine, creating a stunning visual display called 'The River of Gold'.

New areas are being developed too, like the long dell in Witcher's Wood, which gives a lovely deep vista in what to some extent has been the Cinderella of the woods at Exbury in recent years. Tom also hopes to plant more species of rhododendrons near this area as new species are still being found. Lionel had at least one of everything (except R. afghanicum, which he regarded as too 'poisonous') but this is now no longer either the case or the aim; more would, however, be a worthwhile addition. Another new feature is the planting of 48 cherry trees given to Exbury under the UK-Japan Sakura Cherry Tree Project ('Sakura' means 'flowering cherry' or 'cherry blossom' in Japanese); these lovely trees with their distinctive pink flowers have been planted in the picnic area.

Exbury has a dedicated team of gardeners who work throughout the year to ensure the gardens are looking their best; many have worked for much of their lives at Exbury. In addition, a thriving group of volunteers takes on specific roles, including the maintenance of the Herbaceous Borders; other volunteers do labelling, photography and nature conservation.

The twenty-first century advances with new technology, global transformation and environmental challenges, but it is reassuring to know that Exbury Gardens continues to give pleasure to those who visit the peace and tranquillity of its 200 acres. Many return year after year, whether to see the flowers or for peaceful reflection, a good walk in the fresh air or family fun: whatever the reason, Exbury aims to be a place to cherish. While the gardens are in many ways timeless, they too have to move with the times as was demonstrated by Marie-Louise Agius' use of a drone-mounted camera during the Covid lockdown to take dramatic aerial photographs of the gardens in their different moods. She also featured the Agius cockapoo hidden in a series of photographs posted under the name 'Where's Willow Wednesday'. Once the lockdown ended, the gardens were opened again and people clearly appreciated the sense of space and safe environment that Exbury provided.

It gives the present family enormous pleasure to see the gardens being enjoyed by so many people throughout the seasons as the years go by. In the hands of his descendants and the team at Exbury, the enduring legacy of one man, Lionel de Rothschild, would seem to be secure.

When Lionel created Exbury Gardens in only two decades, one contemporary was moved to call it 'the eighth wonder of the world'. To many of its visitors and, especially, to lovers of rhododendrons everywhere, it still is.

194

opposite · *Wisteria floribunda* 'Macrobotrys' in the Sundial Garden

A place to cherish · Exbury today and beyond

PLANT PORTRAITS

196

inside cover
Platanus orientalis

Chapter 1, *page 16*
Blue water lilies, *Nymphaea nouchali var. caerulea*

Chapter 2, *page 34*
A deciduous azalea from
the Exbury range

Chapter 3, *page 48*
M. dawsoniana

Chapter 4, *page 58*
R. Naomi Group

Chapter 5, *page 80*
Enkianthus campanulatus

Chapter 6, *page 102*
R. calophytum, introduced by
Ernest Wilson in 1904

Chapter 7, *page 126*
R. 'Quaver"

Chapter 8, *page 140*
R. quinquefolium 'Five Arrows'

Chapter 9, *page 152*
M. 'Black Tulip'

Chapter 10, *page 180*
Lachenalia quadricolor

page 14
View of Exbury House looking
across to the Isle of Wight

page 28
The Temple at Gunnersbury

page 54
Exbury village in the New Forest,
1906

page 76
The view from Mrs Lionel's
seat in autumn

page 94
Home Wood cascades
in autumn

page 108
M. campbellii, described by
Joseph Hooker in 1855

page 136
One of the large cedars in the Glade,
and Lionel's memorial

page 200
Sunrise over Exbury

ACKNOWLEDGEMENTS

We would like to thank the many people who provided information, answered queries or gave general support. First and foremost comes Thomas Clarke, the head gardener at Exbury Gardens, and his team, all who work in other capacities there and all the volunteers. We hope this book will encourage people to visit, tell others, and visit again. Our thanks also go to the following individuals: Tim Amsden, John Anderson, Steven and Yvonne Betteridge, Michele Blagg, the Hon. Evelyn Boscawen, Val Bott, Trixie Brabner, Alexandra Caccamo, Kenneth Cox, Edwina Elbers, Vanda Foster, Tace Fox, Mark Griffiths, Douglas Harris, Pam Hayward, Nigel Higgins, Jean Hillier, Jennifer Jacobs, Kathryn Johnson, Rosemary Jury, Alison Kenny, Marianna Kneller, Michael and Beverley Lear, Rosemary Legrand, Ruary Mackenzie Dodds and Kari de Koenigswarter, Sally McIntosh, David Millais, Averil Milligan, Charles Nelson, Seamus O'Brien, Vaughan O'Grady, Emma Page, Leonie Paterson, Nigel Philpott, Sophie Piebenga, Catherine Taylor, Neil Porteus, Peter Sander, Andrewjohn and Eleni Stephenson Clarke, Fay and Geoffrey Thornton, and Charles Williams.

We wish to acknowledge our gratitude to a number of archives, gardens and institutions. First and foremost comes The Rothschild Archive, London, its Director, Melanie Aspey, and all its staff; we hope this book may encourage others to use this peerless resource. Our thanks also go to the following institutions: the Arnold Arboretum of Harvard University, the Buckinghamshire Gardens Trust, the Centre for Buckinghamshire Studies, *Country Life*, Gunnersbury Park & Museum, the Hampshire Record Office, Harrow School, the National Botanic Gardens of Ireland, the Royal Archives, the Royal Botanic Garden Edinburgh, the Royal Botanic Gardens, Kew, the Royal Geographical Society, the Royal Horticultural Society libraries at Vincent Square and Wisley, Villa Carlotta, and the Waddesdon Archive.

Francesca's personal thanks go to Peter and their children, her parents and Eileen Beier. My personal thanks go my children, Elizabeth, Leo and Amschel. While Exbury Gardens is above all testament to the extraordinary vision and energy of one man, my grandfather, I know he would have wanted all those who worked with him and after him to be acknowledged too: hopefully this book does exactly that.

Lionel de Rothschild

IMAGE CREDITS

Marie-Louise Agius (*pages*) 2, 10, 14, 34, 79, 87, 89, 90, 122, 125, 126, 131, 136, 140, 145 (*upper right*), 147, 151, 160, 166, 176, 182, 183, 191, 200
John Anderson 4, 58, 75, 92 (*middle*), 115, 157, 163
Melanie Aspey 186, 195
Cathryn Baldock 6, 25, 48, 76, 80, 82, 83, 98, 102, 108, 111, 124, 133, 144, 145 (*lower right*), 150, 152, 162, 164, 171, 178, 180, 192
Kevan Brewer 145 (*lower left*), 174
Gavin Clinton 190
Matthew Cook 182
Lisa Creagh 187, 188
Carole Drake 67 (*lower*)
Nigel Philpott 67 (*upper*), 130, 173, 177
Abigail Rex 158
Colin Roberts 60, 66, 71, 84, 94, 146, 159

Original drawings and paintings by Philadelphia Mitford by kind permission of the Mitford family (*pages*) 50, 56, 57. Other images courtesy of Historic England 85; Arnold Arboretum 119; Royal Botanic Garden Edinburgh 107, 114; Royal Geographical Society 121; Steven Betteridge 168, 169, 170. Remaining images from the collections of The Rothschild Archive and the Rothschild family. We thank those photographers whose names we have inadvertently omitted and apologise to them for any oversight.

Published 2021 by Exbury Gardens Limited

Copyright © 2021 Exbury Gardens Limited

ISBN 978 1 9160402 0 5

EDITORS
Vaughan O'Grady, and Melanie Aspey
DESIGNER Sally McIntosh
PRODUCTION
Produced by Hurtwood, London
Printed and bound in Italy

Sources

ANDREW E. ADAM
Beechwoods & Bayonets: The Book of Halton, Buckinghamshire: Barracuda, 1983

JOHN ANDERSON
A Guide to the Trees of Exbury, Matford: Otter House Ltd, 2012

W.J. BEAN
Trees and Shrubs Hardy in the British Isles, 8th ed., London: John Murray, 1970

VAL BOTT & JAMES WISDOM
Gunnersbury Park: The Place and the People, London: Scala Arts & Heritage Publishers Ltd, 2018

WILLIAM H. BROWN & HAROLD R. FLETCHER
The Royal Botanic Garden Edinburgh, 1670–1970, Edinburgh: Her Majesty's Stationery Office, 1970

ANN & JAMES COLLETT-WHITE
Gunnersbury Park and the Rothschilds, Hounslow: Heritage Publications, 1993

KENNETH COX (ED.)
Frank Kingdon-Ward's Riddle of the Tsangpo Gorges: Retracing the Epic Journey to 1924–25 in South-East Tibet, 2nd rev. ed., Woodbridge: Antique Collectors' Club, 2008

KENNETH COX
Woodland Gardening: Landscaping with Rhododendrons, Magnolias and Camellias and Acid-Loving Plants, Glencarse: Glendoick Publishing, 2018

CYRIL CUNNINGHAM
The Beaulieu River goes to War, 1939–1945, Brockenhurst: Montagu Ventures Limited, 1994

RAY DESMOND
The History of the Royal Botanic Gardens Kew, 2nd ed., London: Royal Botanic Gardens, Kew, 2007

RAY DESMOND
A Celebration of Flowers: Two Hundred Years of Curtis's Botanical Magazine, Kew: Royal Botanic Gardens in association with Collingridge, 1987

BRENT ELLIOTT
'The British Rock Garden in the Twentieth Century', *Occasional Papers from the RHS Lindley Library*, volume 6, London: The RHS Lindley Library, 2011

NIALL FERGUSON
The World's Banker: The History of the House of Rothschild, London: Weidenfeld & Nicholson, 1998

HAROLD R. FLETCHER
The Story of the Royal Horticultural Society, 1804–1968, London: Oxford University Press, 1969

ALGERNON FREEMAN MITFORD
Memories, 2 vols., 2nd ed., London: Hutchinson & Co., 1915

WILLIAM GILPIN
Remarks on Forest Scenery, and other woodland views, (relative chiefly to Picturesque Beauty) illustrated by the scenes of New-Forest in Hampshire …, 2nd ed., London: R. Blamire, 1794

JIM GOODMAN
Joseph F. Rock and his Shangri-La, Hong Kong: Caravan Press, 2006

MARTIN HARPER
Mr Lionel: An Edwardian Episode, London: Cassell, 1970

A.J. HOLLAND & EDMUND DE ROTHSCHILD
Our Exbury: Life in an English Village in the 1920's and early '30's, Southampton: Paul Cave Publications Ltd, 1982

MARK JOHNSTON
Trees in Towns and Cities: A History of British Urban Arboriculture, Oxford: Windgather Press, 2015

MARIANNA KNELLER
The Book of Rhododendrons, Newton Abbot: David and Charles, 1995

ALAN C. LESLIE (compiled)
The International Rhododendron Register & Checklist, 2nd ed., London: Royal Horticultural Society, 2004

CHARLES LYTE
The Royal Gardens in Windsor Great Park, Henley-On-Thames: Aidan Ellis, 1998

BRENDA MCLEAN
George Forrest: Plant Hunter, Woodbridge: Antique Collectors' Club, 2004

RICHARD MILNE
Rhododendron, London: Reaktion Books, 2017

EMMA PAGE
Exbury: The Mitford family's New Forest estate in the 18th century, Lyndhurst: New Forest Heritage Centre, 2018

CYNTHIA POSTAN (ED.)
The Rhododendron Story: 200 years of Plant Hunting and Garden Cultivation, London: The Royal Horticultural Society, 1996

C.E. LUCAS PHILLIPS & PETER N. BARBER
The Rothschild Rhododendrons: A Record of the Gardens at Exbury, 2nd rev. ed., London: Cassell, 1979

MERLE A. REINIKKA
A History of the Orchid, Portland, Oregon: Timber Press, 1995

EDMUND DE ROTHSCHILD
A Gilt-Edged Life, London: John Murray, 1998

MIRIAM ROTHSCHILD
Dear Lord Rothschild: Birds, Butterflies and History, London: Hutchinson, 1983

MIRIAM ROTHSCHILD, KATE GARTON & LIONEL DE ROTHSCHILD
The Rothschild Gardens: A Family Tribute to Nature, London: Gaia Books, 1996

PETER SMITHERS
Adventures of a Gardener, London: Harvill Press with the Royal Horticultural Society, 1995

JOHN STANLEY
The Exbury Junkers: A World War II Mystery, Bognor Regis: Woodfield Publishing, 2004

JUDITH M. TAYLOR
Visions of Loveliness: Great Flower Breeders of the Past, Athens, Ohio: Swallow Press, 2014

Further references to books about the history of the Rothschild family may be found on the website of The Rothschild Archive rothschildarchive.org

The Rothschild Archive Trust is the custodian of the correspondence of Lionel de Rothschild, the primary source on which the text of this book is based, as well as his photographic collections.